REGIONAL INTEGRATION AND SOUTH SUDAN ACCESSION TO THE EAST AFRICAN COMMUNITY

First Edition

Jacob Dut Chol Riak

The publisher wishes to acknowledge and thank Dr. Douglas H. Johnson for his invaluable help and support for Africa World Books and its mission of preserving and promoting African cultural and literary traditions and history. Dr. Johnson and fellow historians have been instrumental in ensuring that African people remain connected to their past and their identity. Africa World Books is proud to carry on this mission.

Cover design, typesetting and layout: Africa World Books
Unit 3, 57 Frobisher St, Osborne Park, WA 6017
P.O. Box 1106 Osbourne Park, WA 6916

DEDICATION

To all South Sudanese who do not know their rights in the East African Community integration - wake up and stand up for those rights!

TABLE OF CONTENTS

List of Tables

List of Figures (Charts)

ACKNOWLEDGEMENT

I am super excited to thank friends and colleagues who helped me to write this book. Thanks to the East African Community (EAC) Secretariat for allowing me to access some data. I am indebted to the Ministry of East African Affairs for providing me with the information I needed during the negotiations of South Sudan's accession to the EAC.

In a special way, I appreciate Africa World Books Press, particularly, CEO, Peter Lual Reec Deng for accepting to publish this book as a historical record for regional integration and South Sudan's accession to the dynamic EAC. I wholeheartedly thank Dr. Sarah Maher for editing the manuscript.

My gratitude will remain incomplete without thanking my dear wife, Rechoh Achol Dau Deng who permitted me to spend time away from her as I wrote and completed this third book in the series of my book publications. Rechoh, I am forever grateful for your understanding and patience!

To all those others who gave a hand in the writing and completion of this book, I sincerely salute you!

ABOUT THE AUTHOR

The author was born on the 3rd May 1983 in Malakal, Upper Nile State, in South Sudan. His father is Abraham Chol Riak Akoi, a retired Police Captain, and his mother is late Daruka Aguet Ajang Duot. Both parents come from Twic East County of Jonglei State. Jacob was conscripted by the SPLA and trained as a child soldier in Dima-Ethiopia military training camp in 1990. He was later passed out after one year of training. He later found his siblings and moved with them to Kapoeta. Within weeks, the enemy from the north captured Kapoeta and Jacob with other child soldiers (also known as Red Army) left for Narus at night.

It was in Narus that Jacob commenced his primary school in 1992. When the war raged on in South Sudan, his family moved to Kakuma Refugee Camp, located in the Turkana District of northwestern Kenya. It is there that Jacob completed his Kenyan Certificate of Primary Education (KCPE) in 1998. Having been amongst the top six best refugee pupils, he won a merit-based scholarship, which was offered by Jesuit Refugee Services (JRS). That scholarship took him to Kakuma Boys High School in 1999. He attended boarding school for four years, subsequently completed secondary education and sat for the Kenyan Certificate of Secondary Education (KCSE).

In 2003, right after completing high school, Jacob worked with

JRS as a Scholarship Desk Officer to give back to the community through community services, especially to thank the Society of Jesus, for being awarded a scholarship. In the same year, he engaged as a youth leader in the camp where he offered a lot of help to many fellow refugees through community mobilization, peace education initiatives, inter-community conflict mitigation programmes, and women's empowerment. In 2004, he worked with the Lutheran World Federation (LWF) as a primary school teacher and later as an editor of the Kakuma News Bulletin (KANEBU), a refugee-based newsletter.

After all these services to the community, Jacob won another scholarship to study an Advanced Diploma in Social Work and Community Development for two years (2005-2007) at Kobujoi Development Training Institute in Nandi Hills, Eldoret, Kenya. He graduated with a Distinction.

In August 2007, he won another scholarship from JRS to study a BA in Social Sciences with double majors in Political Science and Sociology at the Catholic University of Eastern Africa (CUEA) in Nairobi, Kenya. He later graduated with Summa Cum Laude (First Class Honours) on 1st October 2010 for both Sociology and Political Science Degrees. While at CUEA, Jacob served as student leader for both Sudanese Students' Community and University Guild.

Having appeared in Kenyan newspapers as the Best Student in the Faculty of Arts and Social Sciences in October 2010 graduations, Jacob secured another prestigious scholarship in September 2011 from the Africa Educational Trust (AET) that took him to the London School of Economic and Political Science (LSE) to study a MSc in Comparative Politics at the Department of Government. He graduated in 2012 and returned to South Sudan to commence teaching at the University of Juba where he excelled in research and academic writing. In 2014 he enrolled in a PhD programme in Political Science (Comparative Politics) at the University of Juba and graduated in June 2018.

Dr. Jacob Dut Chol Riak is now a renowned international comparative political scientist and seasoned, senior political analyst. He is also an Assistant Professor of International and Comparative Politics and the former Head of Department of Political Science at the University of Juba. He has researched, published and extensively consulted on political theory, democratization and governance, political parties, ethnic politics, violence and spiritual mythology, peace building, mediations and negotiations, regional integration, particular RECS, secessions and secessionist movements, comparative hydro politics, the politics of petroleum, State building and failure in Africa, institutional design in divided societies, human rights as well as small arms surveys in South Sudan.

He is a scholar of the Study of U.S. Institutes (SUSI) on American Political Thought. His articles have appeared in international peer-reviewed journals. He is the author of the two books '*The Birth of States: Successful and Failed Secessions: A Comparative Analysis of South Sudan, Somaliland and Western Sahara*' and '*South Sudan State Formations: Failures, Shocks and Hopes.*' Both books were published by Africa World Books Press, Australia in March and July 2021 respectively.

Dr. Riak is a life member of the Development Policy Forum (DPF), Greater Horn Horizon Forum (GHHF), Council for Development of Social Science Research in Africa (CODESRIA), African Peace Building Network (APN), Institute of Security Studies (ISS), Nordic African Institute (NAI), American Political Science Association (APSA) and the International Political Science Association (IPSA) amongst others.

Dr. Riak is the founder and the Executive Director of the Centre for Democracy and International Analysis (CDIA) registered as a research and academic think-tank in Juba. CDIA does policy design and research on good governance and democratization in South Sudan and Africa.

He is currently the advisor of South Sudan Accession to Regional Economic Communities (RECs).

ACRONYMS AND ABBREVIATIONS

ACP: African, Caribbean & Pacific States

AEC: African Economic Community

AET: African Educational Trust

AMU: Arab Maghreb Union

APSA: American Political Science Association

ASEAN: Association of East Asian Nations

CANS: Civil Authority of New Sudan

CARICOM: Caribbean Community

CASSOA: Civil Aviation Safety and Security Oversight Agency

CDIA: Centre for Democracy and International Analysis

CEEC: Central and Eastern European Countries

CEN: Customs Enforcement Network

CENTO: Central Treaty Organization

CENSAD: Community of Sahel Saharan States

CEO: Chief Executive Officer

CoMs: Council of Ministers

COMESA: Common Market for Eastern and Southern Africa

CMA: Customs Management Act

CMP: Customs Market Protocol

CUEA: Catholic University of Eastern Africa

EA: East Africa

EAC: East African Community

EACA: East African Competition Authority

EACHRC: East African Centre for Health Research Commission

EACJ: East African Court of Justice

EACSO: East African Common Organization

EAHC: East African High Commission

EAKC: East African Kiswahili Commission

EALA: East African Legislative Assembly

EASTECO: East African Science and Technology Organization

EC: European Commission

EEC: European Economic Community

ECCAS: Economic Community of Central African States

ECSC: European Coal and Steel Community

EDF: European Development Fund

EPA: Economic Partnership Agreement

EPZ: Export Processing Zone

EU: European Union

DRC: Domestic Republic of Congo

FCCS: Fears, Concerns & Challenges

FDI: Foreign Direct Investment

ICT: Information Communication Technology

IGAD: Inter-Governmental Authority on Development

IPSA: International Political Science Association

IUCEA: Inter-University Council of East Africa

JRS: Jesuit Refugees Service

KANEBU: Kakuma News Bulletin

KCPE: Kenya Certificate of Primary Education

KCSE: Kenya Certificate of Secondary Education

LVBC: Lake Victoria Basin Commission

LVFO: Lake Victoria Fisheries Organization

LWF: Lutheran World Federation

MOU: Memorandum of Understanding

MRAs: Mutual Recognition Agreements

MUP: Monetary Union Protocol

NAFTA: North America Free Trade Agreement

NAI: Nordic African Institute

NATO: North Atlantic Treaty Organization

NTBs: Non Trade Barriers

OAS: Organization of American States

OAU: Organization of African Unity

OCT: Overseas Countries & Territories

OECD: Organization for Economic Cooperation and Development

PAFTA: Pacific Asia Free Area

RECs: Regional Economic Communities

REPAs: Regional Economic Partnership Agreements

RSS: Republic of South Sudan

RTAs: Regional Trade Agreements

SADC: Southern Africa Development Community

SEATO: Southeast Asia Treaty Organization

SPS: Sanitary Phytosanitary

TANCIS: Tanzania Customs Integrated System

UNCTAD: United Nations Conference for Trade and Development

WCO: World Customs Organization

WTO: World Trade Organization

Map of East African Community

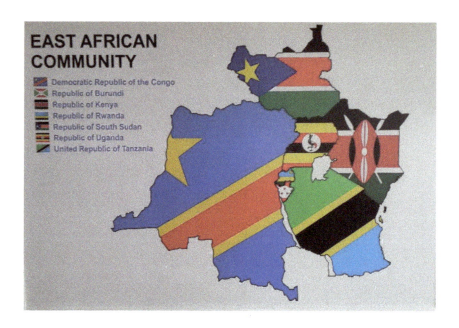

Source: East African Community Secretariat

CHAPTER ONE

Introduction to the East African Community

The East African Community (EAC) is the regional intergovernmental organization of the Republics of Burundi, Kenya, Rwanda, the United Republic of Tanzania, the Republic of Uganda, the Republic of South Sudan and the Democratic Republic of Congo (DRC). It has its headquarters in Arusha, Tanzania. These countries have a population of about 312 million people, potentially providing a rich market for goods and services, which in turn could boost trade and development in the region.

The Treaty for Establishment of the East African Community was signed on 30th November 1999 and entered into force on 7th July 2000 following its ratification by the original three-partner states - Kenya, Tanzania and Uganda. The Republic of Rwanda and the Republic of Burundi acceded to EAC Treaty on 18 June 2007 and became full members of the community with effect from 1 July 2007.

In 2008, after negotiations with the Southern African Development Community (SADC) and the Common Market for Eastern and Southern Africa (COMESA), the EAC agreed to an expanded free trade area including the member states of all three organizations. The EAC is an integral part of the African Economic Community (AEC).

Vision of EAC

A prosperous, competitive, secure, stable and politically united East Africa.

Mission of EAC

To widen and deepen economic, political, social and cultural integration in order to improve the quality of life of the people of East Africa through increased competitiveness, value added production, trade and investments.

EAC's Core Values

- Professionalism
- Accountability
- Transparency
- Teamwork
- Unity in Diversity
- Allegiance to EAC ideals

The Goals of the East African Community

The EAC aims at widening and deepening cooperation among the partner states in, among others, political, economic and social fields for their mutual benefit. To this extent, the EAC countries established Custom Union in 2005, Common Market in 2010 and Monetary Union in 2013. The next and final phase of the integration will see the bloc enter into the Political Federation of the East African States.

Objectives of the East African Community (EAC)

According to Article 5 of the Treaty, the objectives of the EAC are as below:

I.   To develop policies and programmes aimed at widening and deepening co-operation among the Partner States in political, economic, social and cultural fields, research and technology, defence, security and legal and judicial affairs, for their mutual benefit.

II. In pursuance of the provisions of paragraph 1 of this Article, the Partner States undertake to establish among themselves and in accordance with the provisions of this Treaty, a Customs Union, a Common Market, subsequently a Monetary Union and ultimately a Political Federation in order to strengthen and regulate the industrial, commercial, infrastructural, cultural, social, political and other relations of the Partner States to the end that there shall be accelerated, harmonious and balanced development and sustained expansion of economic activities, the benefit of which shall be equitably shared.

III. For purposes set out in paragraph 1 of this Article and as subsequently provided in particular provisions of this Treaty, the Community shall ensure:

   a.   The attainment of sustainable growth and development of the Partner States by the promotion of a more balanced and harmonious development of the Partner States;

   b.   The strengthening and consolidation of co-operation in agreed fields that would lead to equitable economic development within the Partner States and which would in turn, raise the standard of living and improve the quality of life of their populations;

   c.   The promotion of sustainable utilization of the natural resources of the Partner States and the taking of measures that would effectively protect the natural environment of the Partner States;

d. The strengthening and consolidation of the long standing political, economic, social, cultural and traditional ties and associations between the peoples of the Partner States so as to promote a people-centered mutual development of these ties and associations;

e. The mainstreaming of gender in all its endeavors and the enhancement of the role of women in cultural, social, political, economic and technological development;

f. The promotion of peace, security, and stability within, and good neighborliness among, the Partner States;

g. The enhancement and strengthening of partnerships with the private sector and civil society in order to achieve sustainable socio-economic and political development; and

h. The undertaking of such other activities calculated to further the objectives of the Community, as the Partner States may from time to time decide to undertake in common.

Fundamental Principles of the East African Community

According to Article 6 of the Treaty, the fundamental principles that shall govern the achievement of the objectives of the East African Community by the Partner States include:

a. Mutual trust, political will and sovereign equality;

b. Peaceful co-existence and good neighborliness;

c. Peaceful settlement of disputes;

d. Good governance including adherence to the principles of democracy, the rule of law, accountability, transparency, social justice, equal opportunities, gender equality, as well as the recognition, promotion and protection of human and peoples rights in accordance with the provisions of the African Charter on Human and Peoples' Rights;

e. Equitable distribution of benefits; and

f. Co-operation for mutual benefit.

Operational Principles of the Community

According to Article 7 of the Treaty, the principles that govern the practical achievement of the objectives of the Community include:

a. People-centered and market-driven cooperation;

b. The provision by the Partner States of an adequate and appropriate enabling environments, such as conducive policies and basic infrastructure;

c. The establishment of an export-oriented economy for the Partner States in which there shall be free movement of goods, persons, labour, services, capital, information and technology;

d. The principle of subsidiarity with emphasis on multi- level participation and the involvement of a wide range of stake- holders in the process of integration;

e. The principle of variable geometry which allows for progression in co-operation among groups within the Community for wider integration schemes in various fields and at different speeds;

f. The equitable distribution of benefits accruing or to be derived from the operations of the Community and measures to address economic imbalances that may arise from such operations;

g. The principle of complementarity; and

h. The principle of asymmetry.

The Partner States undertake to abide by the principles of good governance, including adherence to the principles of democracy, the rule of law, social justice and the maintenance of universally accepted standards of human rights. However, the practice has been quite abysmal for the Partner States. None of them has achieved in totality, the fundamental and operational principles of the Community.

Major Institutions of EAC Include the Following:

a. The Summit of Heads of State and Government;

b. The Council of Ministers;

c. The Co-ordination Committee;

d. Sectoral Committees;

e. The East African Court of Justice;

f. The East African Legislative Assembly;

g. The Secretariat; and

h. Such other organs as may be established by the Summit.

a. The Summit of Heads of States and Governments

The summit consists of the Heads of State or Government of the Partner States. If a member of the Summit is unable to attend a meeting of the Summit and it is not convenient to postpone the meeting, that member may, after consultation with other members of the Summit, appoint a Minister of Government to attend the meeting. A Minister so appointed shall, for purposes of that meeting, have all the powers, duties and responsibilities of the member of the Summit for whom that person is acting.

Functions of the Summit of the Heads of State and Government

i. The Summit gives general directions and impetus as to the development and achievement of the objectives of the Community.

ii. The Summit considers the annual progress reports and such other reports submitted to it by the Council as provided for by the Treaty.

iii. The Summit review the state of peace, security and good governance within the Community and the progress achieved towards the establishment of a Political Federation of the Partner States.

iv. The Summit may have such other functions as may be conferred upon it by this Treaty of the community.

v. Subject to EAC Treaty, the Summit can delegate the exercise of any of its functions, subject to any conditions, which it may think fit to impose, to a member of the Summit, to the Council or to the Secretary General.

vi. An Act of the Community may provide for the delegation of any powers, including legislative powers, conferred on the Summit by the EAC Treaty or by any Act of the Community, to the Council or to the Secretary General.

vii. Subject to the provisions of any Act of the Community, the acts and decisions of the Summit may be signified under the hand of the Secretary General or of any officer in the service of the Community authorized in that behalf by the Summit.

viii.The Summit shall cause all rules and orders made by it under the Treaty to be published in the Gazette; and any such rules or orders shall come into force on the date of publication unless otherwise provided in the rule or order.

ix. The delegation of powers and functions referred to in paragraphs v and vi of this Article, shall not include:

I. The giving of general directions and impetus;

II. The appointment of Judges to the East African Court of Justice;

III.The admission of new Members and granting of Observer Status to foreign countries; and

IV. Assent to Bills.

b. Council of Ministers (CoMs)

As stipulated in the EAC Treaty, the Council shall consist of the Ministers responsible for regional co-operation of each Partner State and such other Ministers of the Partner States as each Partner State may determine. The CoMs has the following functions:

I. It is the policy organ of the Community;

II. It promotes, monitors and keeps under constant review the implementation of the programmes of the Community and ensures the proper functioning and development of the Community in accordance with the Treaty.

III. For purposes of paragraph I, the CoMs):

    i. Makes policy decisions for the efficient and harmonious functioning and development of the Community;

    ii. Initiates and submit Bills to the Assembly;

    iii. Subjects to the EAC Treaty, give directions to the Partner States and to all other organs and institutions of the Community other than the Summit, Court and the Assembly;

    iv. Makes regulations, issue directives, take decisions, make recommendations and give opinions in accordance with the provisions of the Treaty;

    v. Considers the budget of the Community;

    vi. Considers measures that should be taken by Partner States in order to promote the attainment of the objectives of the Community;

    vii. Makes staff rules and regulations and financial rules and regulations of the Community;

    viii. Submits annual progress reports to the Summit and prepare the agenda for the meetings of the Summit;

    ix. Establishes from among its members, Sectoral Councils to deal with such matters that arise under the Treaty as the Council may delegate or assign to them and the decisions of such Sectoral Councils shall be deemed to be decisions of the Council;

    x. Establishes the Sectoral Committees provided for under the Treaty;

    xi. Implements the decisions and directives of the Summit as may be addressed to it;

xii. Endeavors to resolve matters that may be referred to it; and

xiii. Exercises such other powers and performs such other functions as are vested in or conferred on it by the Treaty.

IV. The Council may request advisory opinions from the Court in accordance with the Treaty.

V. The Council shall cause all regulations and directives made or given by it under the Treaty to be published in the Gazette; and such regulations or directives shall come into force on the date of publication unless otherwise provided therein.

c. The Coordination Committee

The co-ordination committee consists of the permanent secretaries/undersecretaries responsible for regional co-operation in each partner state and such other permanent secretaries/undersecretaries of the partner states as each partner state may determine.

Functions of the Co-ordination Committee

In accordance with the EAC Treaty, the Co-ordination Committee performs the following functions:

I. Submits from time to time, reports and recommendations to the Council either on its own initiative or upon the request of the Council, on the implementation of the Treaty;

II. Implement the decisions of the Council as the Council may direct;

III. Receives and considers reports of the Sectoral Committees and co-ordinate their activities;

IV. Requests a Sectoral Committee to investigate any particular matter; and

V. Have such other functions as are conferred upon it by the Treaty.

d. The Sectoral Committees

The co-ordination committee shall recommend to the Council the establishment; composition and functions of such sectoral committees as may be necessary for the achievement of the objectives of the Treaty.

Functions of the Sectoral Committees

Subject to any directions the Council may give, each Sectoral Committee should perform as follows:

I.   Be responsible for the preparation of a comprehensive implementation programme and the setting out of priorities with respect to its sector;

II. Monitors and keep under constant review the implementation of the programmes of the Community with respect to its sector;

III. Submits from time to time, reports and recommendations to the Co-ordination Committee either on its own initiative or upon the request of the Co-ordination Committee concerning the implementation of the provisions of the Treaty that affect its sector; and

IV. Have such other functions as may be conferred on it by or under the Treaty.

e. The East African Court of Justice (EACJ)

The Court is a judicial body, which is mandated to administer justice and ensures the adherence to law in the interpretation and application of and compliance with the EAC Treaty.

Judges of the Court

I.   Judges of the Court are appointed by the Summit from among persons recommended by the Partner States who are of proven integrity, impartiality and independence and who fulfill the conditions required in their own countries for the holding of such high judicial office, or who are jurists of recognized competence, in their respective Partner States: provided that no more than two Judges shall at any time be appointed on the recommendation of the same Partner State.

II. The number of Judges of the Court shall be a maximum of six: Provided that of the Judges first appointed to the Court, the terms of two Judges shall expire at the end of five years, the terms of two other Judges shall expire at the end of six years and the remaining two Judges shall serve their full term of seven years.

III. The Judges whose terms are to expire at the end of each of the initial periods mentioned in paragraph 2 of the Article shall be chosen by lot to be drawn by the Summit immediately after their first appointment.

IV. There shall be a President and a Vice President of the Court who shall be appointed by the Summit from among the Judges appointed under paragraph 1 of the Article: Provided that the President and the Vice President of the Court were not recommended for appointment by the same Partner State.

V. The office of President of the Court shall be held in rotation after the completion of any one term.

VI. The President of the Court shall direct the work of the Court, represent it, regulate the disposition of matters brought before the Court, and preside over its sessions.

f. The East African Legislative Assembly (EALA)

Membership of the Assembly

The members of the Assembly comprise of the following:

a. Fifty-four elected members; and

b. Eight ex-officio members consisting of:
    i.   The Minister responsible for regional co- operation from each Partner State; and
    ii. The Secretary General and the Counsel to the Community.

The Speaker of the Assembly shall preside over and take part in its proceedings in accordance with the rules of procedure of the Assembly.

The Assembly shall have committees which shall be constituted in the manner provided in the rules of procedure of the Assembly and shall perform the functions provided in respect thereof in the said rules of procedure.

The Council shall appoint a Clerk of the Assembly and other officers of the Assembly whose salaries and other terms and conditions of service shall be determined by the Council.

Functions of the EALA

I.   The Assembly shall be the legislative organ of the Community.
II. The Assembly shall:
     a. Liaise with the National Assemblies of the Partner States on matters relating to the Community;
     b. Debate and approve the budget of the Community;
     c. Consider annual reports on the activities of the Community, annual audit reports of the Audit Commission and any other reports referred to it by the Council;
     d. Discuss all matters pertaining to the Community and make recommendations to the Council as it may deem necessary for the implementation of the Treaty;
     e. For purposes of carrying out its functions, establish any committee or committees for such purposes as it deems necessary;

f.   Recommend to the Council the appointment of the Clerk and other officers of the Assembly; and

g.   Make its rules of procedure and those of its committees.

h.   Perform any other functions as are conferred upon it by the Treaty.

g. The Secretariat

Establishment of the Secretariat

The Secretariat shall be the executive organ of the Community. There shall be the following offices in the service of the Community:

a.   Secretary General;

b.   Deputy Secretaries General;

c.   Counsel to the Community; and

d.   Such other offices as may be deemed necessary by the Council.

Secretary General

The Secretary General shall be appointed by the Summit upon nomination by the relevant Head of State under the principle of rotation.

Upon the appointment of the Secretary General the Partner State from which he or she is appointed shall forfeit the post of Deputy Secretary General.

The Secretary General shall be the principal executive officer of the Community and shall:

a.   Be the head of the Secretariat

b.   Be the Accounting Officer of the Community

c.   Be the Secretary of the Summit; and

d.   Carry out such other duties as are conferred upon him by the Treaty or by the Council from time to time.

The Secretary General shall serve a fixed five-year term. The terms and conditions of service of the Secretary General shall be determined by the Council and approved by the Summit.

Deputy Secretaries General

The Council shall determine the number of Deputy Secretaries General as follows.

a. The Deputy Secretaries General shall be appointed by the Summit on recommendations of the Council and on a rotational basis.

b. The Deputy Secretaries General shall:

    i. Deputize for the Secretary General; and

    ii. Perform such other duties as may be prescribed by the Council.

c. The Deputy Secretaries General shall each serve a three-year term, renewable once.

The terms and conditions of service of the Deputy Secretaries General shall be determined by the Council and approved by the Summit.

Counsel to the Community

There shall be a Counsel to the Community who shall be the principal legal adviser to the Community. The Counsel to the Community shall perform such duties as are conferred upon him or her by the Treaty and by the Council.

The Counsel to the Community shall be appointed on contract and in accordance with the staff rules and regulations and terms and conditions of service of the Community.

The other terms and conditions of service of the Counsel to the Community shall be determined by the Council.

Table 1: EAC Organs and Institutions

S/no	Institution	Location
1.	EAC Secretariat (HQ)	Ausha, Tanzania
2.	Lake Victoria Basin Commission (LVBC)	Kisumu, Kenya
3.	Inter University Council for East Africa (IUCEA)	Kampala, Uganda
4.	East African Competition Authority (EACA)	Ausha, Tanzania
5.	Civil Aviation Safety and Security Oversight Agency (CASSOA)	Entebbe, Uganda
6.	East African Kiswahili Commission (EAKC)	Zanzibar, Tanzania
7.	Lake Victoria Fisheries Organization (LVFO)	Jinja, Uganda
8.	East African Legislative Assembly (EALA)	Arusha, Tanzania
9.	East African Court of Justice (EACJ)	Ausha, Tanzania
10.	East African Science & Technology Organization (EASTECO)	Kigali, Rwanda
11.	East African Centre for Health Research Commission (EACHRC)	Bujumbura, Burundi

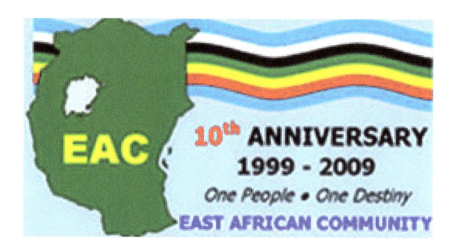

Motto of EAC: **'One People. One Destiny'**
Source: EAC Secretariat

EAC Passport   *EAC Flag*

EAC Emblem

EAC Anthem

[1]
Ee Mungu twaomba ulinde
Jumuiya Afrika Mashariki
Tuwezeshe kuishi kwa amani
Tutimize na malengo yetu.

[Chorus]
Jumuiya Yetu sote tuilinde
Tuwajibike tuimarike
Umoja wetu ni nguzo yetu
Idumu Jumuiya yetu.

[2]
Uzalendo pia mshikamano
Viwe msingi wa Umoja wetu
Natulinde Uhuru na Amani
Mila zetu na desturi zetu.

[3]
Viwandani na hata mashambani
Tufanye kazi sote kwa makini
Tujitoe kwa hali na mali
Tuijenge Jumuiya bora.

Etymology and Re-etymology of East African Community (EAC)

Kenya, Tanzania, and Uganda have cooperated with each other since the early 20th century. The East African Currency Board provided a common currency from 1919 to 1966. The customs union between Kenya and Uganda in 1917, which Tanganyika joined in 1927 and was followed by the East African High Commission (EAHC) from 1948 to 1961, the East African Common Services Organization (EACSO) from 1961 to 1967, and the EAC from 1967 to 1977. Burundi and Rwanda joined the EAC on 18th June 2007.

Inter-territorial co-operation between the Kenya Colony, the Uganda Protectorate, and the Tanganyika Territory was formalized in 1948 by the EAHC. This provided the customs union, a common external tariff, currency, and postage. It also dealt with common services in transport and communications, research, and education. Following independence, these integrated activities were reconstituted and the EAHC was replaced by the EACSO, which many observers thought would lead to a political federation between the three territories. The new organization ran into difficulties because of the lack of joint planning and fiscal policy, separate political policies, and Kenya's dominant economic position. In 1967, the EACSO was superseded by the EAC. This body aimed to strengthen the ties between the members through a common market, a common customs tariff, and a range of public services to achieve balanced economic growth within the region. Indeed, EAC was in operation from 1967 as cooperation when the Treaty establishing it was signed until 1977 when the then cooperation collapsed after 10 years of existence. In 1984, mediation agreement was signed for division of assets and liabilities amongst the three founding partner states of Kenya, Uganda and Tanzania.

Why did the Cooperation Collapse in 1977?

The cooperation collapsed due to the following reasons:

a. Ideological differences between Kenya and Tanzania whereby the former preferred capitalism while the latter preferred socialism/ ujamma/vilagelization

b. Hatred between Mzee Jomo Kenyatta and Mwalimu Julius Nyerere

c. Intra-community political differences: Kenya demanded more seats than Uganda and Tanzania in decision-making organs, disagreements with Ugandan dictator Idi Amin who demanded that Tanzania as a member state of the EAC should not harbor forces fighting to topple the government of another member state, and the disparate economic systems of socialism in Tanzania and capitalism in Kenya.

d. Kagera war between Uganda and Tanzania from October 1978 to June 1979 in which the former was defeated. The war was preceded by a deterioration of relations between Uganda and Tanzania following Amin's 1971 overthrow of President Milton Obote who was close to the President of Tanzania, Julius Nyerere. The war led to the overthrowing of Idi Amin and later a Uganda bush war broke out.

e. Differences in sharing benefits from jointly owned common services organization and lack of policy to redress the situation: The three member states lost over sixty years of co-operation and the benefits of economies of scale, although some Kenyan government officials celebrated the collapse with champagne.

f. The then East/West divide

g. Low private sector and civil society input in the running of the then community.

h. Greed and short-sightedness on the part of some influential leaders in East Africa

i. East-West Foreign Policy influence

Nonetheless, Presidents Daniel Torotich Arap Moi of Kenya, Ali Hassan Mwinyi of Tanzania, and Yoweri Kaguta Museveni of Uganda signed the Treaty for East African Co-operation in Kampala on 30th November 1993 and established a Tri-partite Commission for Co-operation. A process of re-integration was embarked on involving tripartite programmes of co-operation in political, economic, social and cultural fields, research and technology, defence, security, and legal and judicial affairs.

The East African Cooperation was revived on 30 November 1999, when the treaty for its re-establishment was signed and later changed to the East African Community (EAC). It came into force on 7 July 2000, 23 years after the collapse of the previous community and its organs. A customs union was signed in March 2004, which commenced on 1 January 2005. Kenya, the region's largest exporter, continued to pay duties on goods entering the other four countries on a declining scale until 2010. A common system of tariffs would apply to goods imported from third-party countries. On 30 November 2016 it was declared that the immediate aim for the EAC would be confederation rather than federation.

The treaty forming the East African Community, signed on the 30th of November 1999, sets out the following with regard to economic integration:

> "[the EAC members are]…determined to strengthen their economic, social, cultural, political, technological, and other ties for the fast, balanced and sustainable development by the establishment of an East African Community, with an East African Customs Union, and a Common Market as transitional stages to and integral parts thereof, subsequently a Monetary Union and ultimately a Political Federation."

*East African Heads of States Signed the Treaty for
the Establishment of EAC, 30 November 1999*

The goal of the current EAC is not limited to the economic sphere. EAC Treaty, integration includes development of;

"Policies and programmes aimed at widening and deepening cooperation among the Partner States in political, economic, social and cultural fields, research and technology, defense, security and legal and judicial affairs, for their mutual benefit".

Table 2: EAC Current Partner States

Country	Capital	Accession	Population	Area (km²)
Uganda	Kampala	2000	50,770,775	241,550
Tanzania	Dodoma	2000	67,273,474	945,087
Kenya	Nairobi	2000	56,517,268	580,367
Burundi	Gitega	2007	12,800,008	27,834
Rwanda	Kigali	2007	13,766,468	26,338
South Sudan	Juba	2016	14,433,660	644,329
DR Congo	Kinshasa	2022	96,801,000	2,344,858
			312,362,653	4,810,363

Source: EAC Portal, 2022

Emerging Business Trends in EAC

Business leaders are far more positive than economists about the benefits of EAC integration, its customs union as a step in the process, as
well as the wider integration under COMESA. The larger economic
players perceive long-term benefits in a progressively expanding
regional market. Patterns of regional development are already emerging, including:

- Kenyan firms have successfully aligned to the lower protection
  afforded by the EAC CET and fears that firms would not adjust to
  a 25% maximum CET, or would relocate to Tanzania or Uganda
  have not been realized.

- An intra-regional division of labor is developing, which results
  in basic import-processing relocating to the coast to supply the
  hinterland. The final stages of import-processing (especially those
  bulky finished goods that involve high transportation costs) and
  natural-resource based activities are moving up-country and
  up-region, either within value chains of large companies or different segments located by firms in different countries.

- Trade in goods and services has already increased as services provision to Kenyans and Tanzanians are already important for Uganda
  (in education and in health). Kenya exports financial services,
  for example via the Kenya Commercial Bank and it engages in
  upgrading and promoting of local operators in Tanzania, Uganda
  and South Sudan. Uganda hopes integration will help support its
  tourism potential through integration with established regional
  circuits.

- There are signs of a business culture oriented to making profits
  through economies of scale and not from protectionism.

CHAPTER TWO

Theories of Regional Integration

Empirical studies on regionalism and economic integration has made it clear that economic, geopolitical and socio-cultural relationships across the globe, for which Africa is no exception, have been changing rapidly in the last few decades. The world has seen a dramatic increase in Regional Trade Agreements (RTAs) since the early 1990s. Although there were only 124 RTAs notifications before 1995, this number rose to 625 by July 31, 2021, out of which 409 were in force (WTO Report, 2021). International trade, foreign direct investment, international migration, technology transfer, international politics, and policy coordination have been key forces behind this trend of increasingly close cooperation among member countries of regional and economic blocs. Economically, regionalism and economic integration among nations is anticipated to increase the chances for investment, be useful to the people of the nations, and foster exploration of growth and development resources (Asante-Poku and Angelucci, 2013). This is really good news for African countries where growth and development agenda have been key in the last few decades, particularly in light of the continent's desire to achieve the United Nations' Sustainable Development Goals by 2030.

It is interesting to note that although the two concepts—regionalism and economic integration—are often used interchangeably; they are not necessarily the same thing. While regionalism is much broader and involves forming entities of countries with shared political, economic, social, cultural, and geographical demarcations, economic integration is often considered within the framework of economic theory (for example the contribution of economic theory to understanding the economic aspect of regionalism). This was the character of the creation of regionalism in most parts of the world (and Europe in particular) after the post–Cold War era (Soderbaum, 2004) although the instigation of formal regionalism can be dated to the late nineteenth or early twentieth century (Capoccia and Ziblatt, 2010). Integration has multiple meanings for different actors in diverse contexts. To integrate means to bring together for common good. Regional integration refers to bringing the region (countries in the region) together.

Early post-war regionalism across the globe comprised three main categories:

i.   Security regionalism, such as the North Atlantic Treaty Organization (NATO), Southeast Asia Treaty Organization (SEATO), and Central Treaty Organization (CENTO);

ii. Economic regionalism, such as the European Commission (EC), North American Free Trade Agreement (NAFTA), Pacific Asia Free Trade Area (PAFTA), Economic Community of West African States (ECOWAS), Economic Community of Central African States (ECCAS), and Southern African Development Community (SADC); and

iii. Multi-purpose regionalism or organizations, such as the Organization of American States (OAS), the African Union (AU), and League of Arab States (LAS) (Senarclens and Kazancigil, 2007).

Africa's pre-independence history of regionalism and economic integration dates to the early twentieth century, when the South African Customs Union (SACU) was formed. Following political independence, the call for regionalism and economic integration in African countries was renewed during the days of Kwame Nkrumah, the first President of Ghana. After leading Ghana to achieve independence in 1957, Nkrumah attempted to gain political independence as well as economic and political integration for the whole continent. In his speech declaring independence for his country, he said that Ghana's independence was meaningless unless it was linked with the total liberation of Africa and that Ghana's independence was only the first step toward a united and integrated Africa. He shared his vision at Gold Coast Freedom Square in 1957 with a mantra *"seek ye first the political kingdom and all other things shall be added on to you."*

Although Nkrumah did not live to see his dream come to reality, the post-independence period saw many African leaders embracing the concept of regionalism and economic integration as a vital element of their development agenda and engaging their countries in a number of regional and economic integration arrangements. In addition to Nkrumah, leaders such as George Patmore, W.E.B. Dubois, Marcus Garvey, and Julius Nyerere, among others, saw the need for regionalism in Africa, which they thought would quicken the pace of the continent's economic and social development (UNCTAD, 2009).

Africa has adopted regionalism mainly because of its potential economic benefits. As Kales Julian (2012) notes, African leaders have come to realize the benefits of regionalism in stimulating stability and cooperation through inter-regional policies, institution building, trade, and other issues of common interest (Julian, 2012). Moreover, the creation of regional blocs was seen as a way to rescue the continent from colonial and neo-colonial influences and enable it to effectively engage with the developed world. It is not surprising that the continent has for decades initiated a variety of regional arrangements, mainly along economic and political lines, aimed at integrating Africa to achieve these benefits.

One such arrangement is the famous Lagos Plan launched in 1985 by the Organization of African Unity, which was founded in 1963 and succeeded by the African Union in 2002. The Plan envisaged three regional arrangements aimed at the creation of separate but convergent and overarching integration arrangements in three sub-Saharan African sub-regions. West Africa was served by the Economic Community of West African States (ECOWAS), which pre-dated the Lagos Plan. East and Southern Africa were served by the Common Market for Eastern and Southern Africa (COMESA). For Central Africa, the Treaty of the Economic Community of Central African States (ECCAS) was also approved. All these arrangements, together with that of the Arab Maghreb Union (AMU) in North Africa were expected to lead to an all-African common market by the year 2025 (Hartzenberg, 2011).

Several other arrangements have occurred following the Lagos Plan. Among these is the famous Abuja Treaty of 1991, which aimed to reaffirm the commitment of the OAU's heads of states to an integrated African economy. Delineated within this Treaty was the creation of the African Economic Community (AEC), African Monetary Union, African Central Bank, African Court of Justice, and Pan African Parliament. In order to speed up the process of creating these entities, the 1999 Sirte Declaration was signed; which later led to the 2002 launch by African heads of states of the African Union (AU), which replaced the Organization of African Unity (OAU). In addition to those already mentioned, recognized regional and economic integration organizations include the Community of Sahel-Saharan States (CENSAD), the Inter-Governmental Authority on Development (IGAD), the Southern African Development Community (SADC), and the East African Community (EAC).

Regionalism can refer to the efforts by a group of countries to enhance their economic, political, social, or cultural interactions. Lee (2002) argues groups' regionalism as under four major headings: economic (market) integration, regional cooperation, regional integration, and development integration (Lee, 2002).

Economic integration is the commercial policy of discriminatively reducing or eliminating protectionist policies only among participating countries (Salvatore, 2010). It focuses on widening the market of the countries joining together. Phillips Drysdale and Richard Gamaut (1992) define economic integration as a movement toward one price throughout the global economy for goods and services (Drysdale and Gamaut, 1992).

Regional cooperation involves cooperation among distinct countries with a shared interest in a particular issue and may include "the execution of joint projects, technical sector cooperation, common running of services and policy harmonization, and joint development of common natural resources" (Lee, 2002).

Regional integration is "a process whereby political actors in several distinct national settings are persuaded to shift their loyalties, expectations, and political activities toward a new centre, whose institutions possess or demand jurisdiction over the pre-existing national states" (Haas, 1958).

Development integration involves collaboration by a number of distinct countries whose main objective or agenda is the economic and social development of their region. To Lee, this requires more state intervention, as it was seen as a response to the problems created by economic integration, although it has proved more difficult to implement.

Regional cohesion, the greatest form of regionalism, occurs through the combination of all the above regionalism processes. With this, there is the formation of a unified and united regional entity.

Andrea Hurrell (1995) compares new and old regionalism and comes up with five distinctive characteristics of new regionalism, which:

i.   Appears very broad in its scope and has a variety of structures or procedures for forming regionalism;

ii. Does not restrict regionalism or integration among countries just in a particular geographical location or stage of development. It expands to even partnerships between countries on different continents and at different levels of development (among developing and developed countries);

iii. Differs greatly in the level of institutionalization of the different regions;

iv. Presents itself in a multifaceted manner, going beyond a particular focus (be it social or political); and

v.   Entails the formation of a regional sense of identity (Hurrell, 1995).

The discussion of regionalism by Hurrell and Lee reveals some interesting similarities and distinctions. Under Hurrell's classifications, regionalization and regional awareness and identity are not necessarily government-induced. However, all the others—regional interstate cooperation, state-promoted regional integration, regional cohesion, economic integration, regional cooperation, regional integration, and development integration—are mainly government initiatives. While regionalization focuses more on social and economic benefits with more roles for the private sector, regional awareness and identity stresses the importance of identical traits and ideologies among countries. Other than developmental integration and perhaps regional cohesion—which is also founded on both social and economic benefits like regionalization - regional interstate cooperation, state promoted regional integration, and economic integration all place emphasis on economic gains.

Additional definitions cast regionalization as a political process (political union or integration) characterized by economic policy coordination and harmonization among member countries (Fishlow and Haggard, 1992). However, in some situations, regionalism can be viewed as a socio-political project with aspirations to restore past ethnic and cultural identities and autonomies (Giordano, 2000).

What is worrying for regionalism and economic integration in Africa is that, although some efforts have been made, the full rationale for the formation of the AU, AEC, and the eight recognized regional blocs (ECOWAS, COMESA, ECCAS, AMU, CENSAD, IGAD, SADC, and EAC) is yet to be realized.

Apart from African based regional blocs, other regions in North America and Europe formed their own regional organizations. One such organization is European Economic Community (EEC) of 1957 via Treaty of Rome to the European Union formed in the 1960s as the European Coal and Steel Community (ECSC), to The Maastricht Treaty established European Union in 1993 and introduced European Citizenship. The Lisbon Treaty that came to force in 2009 allowed several constitutional amendments to the Maastricht Treaty.

Types of Regional Integration

Preferential Trade Area

Poor countries extend preferential treatment in terms of charging lower tariffs on imports produced in member countries, than they charge on imports from non-member countries.

Free Trade Area

A regime of free trades within the area of which both tariffs and non-tariff barriers (e.g. quota) or administrative barriers are removed – falls short of effective customs union (each member levies its own regime of tariffs on imports from non-members) as agreed on rules of origin.

Customs Union

A customs union develops a regime of external tariffs on goods imported from countries outside the customs union (no unilateral extension of preferential tariffs to non-members) – arises with membership to different regional organizations apart members of the EAC.

Common Market

In addition to what obtains from customs union there is free movement of labor, capital, goods and service amongst member countries – nationals have the right to establish themselves economically in any member country.

Economic Union

In addition to attributes of a common market, it has a higher degree of integration, harmonization and integration of economic policy, fiscal and monetary policy.

Political Union

It's the culmination of the integration process; the member countries can either completely unite or give up all their sovereignty or they may federate or confederate.

Critical Factors in Regional Integration

These factors are discussed as follows:

i. **Common history, language and culture.** Countries will seek to integrate due to the common history, similar language and cultures. This is what the EU, EAC and other Regional Economic Communities (RECS) have done. In the EAC the six partner states have tribes and ethnic groups mingling across their borders. These ethnic groups such as Bantus, Nilotes and Cushitic people are found in Kenya, Uganda, Tanzania, Rwanda, Burundi, South Sudan and DR Congo.

ii. **History of cooperation.** Before the formation of the first East African Cooperation in 1967, there was already cooperation in place in the region. For instance, in 1900, Mombasa was established as a customs collections centre for Uganda and the entire Eastern African region. While the customs collections centre was critical, in 1905, currency board was set up to issue currency for Kenya and Uganda. By 1917, a customs union was established between Kenya and Uganda – Tanganyika joined in 1922. In 1948, the East Africa High Commission was established to serve Uganda, Kenya and Tanzania. Finally in 1961, the Common Services Organisation established East African Posts and Telecommunications, East African Railways & Harbours, East African Airways, East African Air Aviation Services, and the East African Development Bank, for the region.

iii. **Shared natural resources.** In the case of EAC, shared natural resources such as Lake Victoria, the river Nile (and rains in the region), aid in deepening integration as well as widening the cooperation.

iv. **Geographical advantage.** Geographical proximity is key for effective regional integration. This is because the closeness of the countries helps in enhancing trade and easy markets. Thus, EAC countries are bordering each other and this is essential in common trade and security.

v. **Common infrastructural network.** This is very critical for any meaningful integration. For the case of EAC, the roads are being linked amongst the partner states. Common railways such as the EAC standard gauge railway (SGR) and shared power pool such as EAC power pool now being piloted by the Republic of Uganda, Kenya, Tanzania and Rwanda.

Regional Economic Communities (RECs)/Regional Blocks

- November 1993 – the Treaty on the European Union (TEU) -Maastricht Treaty – enlarged and built upon the European Economic Community.
- September 1993 – the North America Free Trade Agreement (NAFTA).
- January 1993 – AFTA (the ASEAN Free Trade Area).
- January 1995 – the Southern Common Market Treaty (MERCOSUR) in Latin America.
- Free Trade Area of the Americas (FTAA).
- Asia-Pacific Economic Cooperation (APEC).
- COMESA – Common Market for Eastern and Southern Africa - Lusaka, Zambia.
- SADC – the Southern African Development Community - Gaborone, Botswana.
- ECOWAS – the Economic Community of Western African States - Abuja, Nigeria.
- IGAD – Inter-governmental Authority on Development - Djibouti, Djibouti.
- ECCAS – Economic Community of Central African States - Libreville, Gabon.
- CEN-SAD-Community of Sahel-Saharan States - Tripoli, Libya.
- AMU/UMA-Arab Maghreb Union - Rabat, Morocco.
- EAC – East African Community - Arusha, Tanzania.
- The Economic Commission for Africa (ECA) supported three regional integration arrangements.
- The Economic Community of West African States (ECOWAS) for West Africa.
- The Preferential Trade Area (PTA) covering East and Southern Africa, which was the precursor of the Common Market for Eastern and Southern Africa (COMESA).

- The Economic Community of Central Africa States (ECCAS) for Central Africa.
- The Arab Maghreb Union (AMU) for North Africa and Middle East.
- The Southern African Development Coordinating Conference (SADCC) 1980 aimed at reducing economic dependence on apartheid South Africa – later became the Southern African Development Community (SADC) in 1992 – envisaged establishment of a free trade area by 2008, a *customs union* in 2010, a common market in 2015, monetary union in 2016 and the introduction of a *single currency* in 2018.
- The East African Community (EAC) was established in 1999. However, ECOWAS in West Africa adopted the linear approach.
- COMESA – aims to become a common market.
- The Southern African Customs Union (SACU) – is an established customs union, with no plans to move beyond this.
- African integration reflects a strong focus on the liberalization of trade in goods, following the provisions of Article XXIV of the General Agreement on Tariffs and Trade (GATT), in the establishment of free trade areas and customs union.

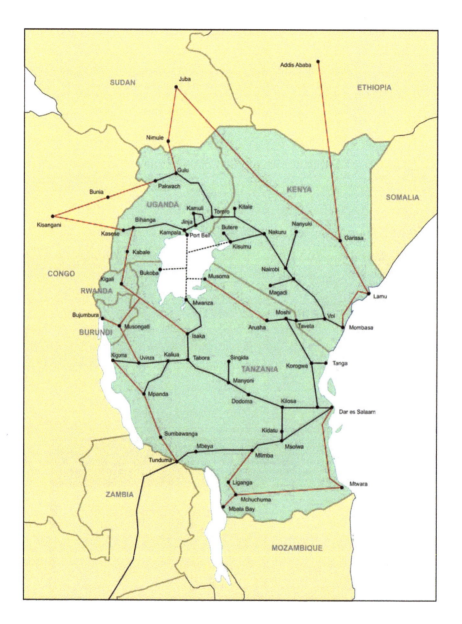

Greater East Africa Roads Network

CHAPTER THREE

The Importance of Regional Integration

Trade and Peace in Regional Integration

The idea that trade between countries can be an important force for creating and maintaining peaceful relations between them is, indeed, an old one. It certainly dates back from the eighteenth century and is probably a good deal older. Given that forming a regional bloc increases trade between the partners, which seems to be a good chance that the pacific effects stretch to this particular form of trade relationship. In fact, this is true only part of the time: when the regional bloc is between relatively evenly balanced partners whose government genuinely wishes to improve security and when the distribution of benefits from the regional bloc is relatively equal.

Trade and Peace: The Political Lineup Follows the Economic Lineup

The notion of using international trade to diffuse tension and bring nations is clear in the 1795 publication of Kant's *Perpetual Peace* (1992). The 19th century British politician Richard Cobden persistently advocated that Britain trade freely with her neighbors to convince them of the advantages of free trade, and as a means of locking them more fully into the community of nations. Cordell Hull, US Secretary of State (1933-44), and one of the architects of the post-war international trading order, advocated this view throughout his public life. For instance, he states "if we could increase commercial exchanges among nations over lowered trade and tariff barriers and remove unnatural obstructions to trade, we would go a long way toward eliminating war itself" (Hull, 1948). And referring to World War I, he states:

> *"Yes, war did come, despite the trade agreements. But it is a fact that war did not break out between the United States and any country with which we had been able to negotiate a trade agreement. ...With very few exceptions, the countries with which we signed trade agreements joined together in resisting the Axis. The political lineup followed the economic lineup" (Ibid).*

Diplomatic considerations were at the heart of the 1860 Anglo-French (Cobden- Chevalier) commercial treaty (Irwin 1992). France was worried about offending protectionist interests, while Britain was somewhat reluctant to pursue an agreement that would violate its policy of unilateral free trade. Nevertheless, both governments saw a commercial treaty as a way of defusing tensions and improving diplomatic relations, and decided to sign it. In 1889, the Italian economist Vilfredo Pareto argued that customs unions were "a means to better political relations and eventual pacification" (Machlup, 1977).

As early as 1943, Frenchman Jean Monnet – one of the founding fathers of the European Economic Community (EEC) - wrote:

> *"There will be no peace in Europe if the states reconstitute themselves on a basis of national sovereignty with its policies of prestige and economic protection ... the constitution of large*

armies will again be necessary ... Europe will once again be recreated in fear ...unless the States of Europe join in a Federation or a 'European entity' that results in a common economic unit"
(Reflexion note, 5 August 1943).

Jean Monnet and Robert Schuman, the other architect of the EEC, were explicit that the precursor of the EEC, the European Coal and Steel Community (ECSC) was to make Franco-German war not only "unthinkable, but materially impossible" (Swann, 1992). The preamble to the 1951 Paris Treaty establishing that Community "resolved to substitute for age old rivalries the merging of their essential interests, [and] to create, by establishing an economic community, the basis for a broader and deeper community among peoples long divided by bloody conflicts" (Swann, 1992). Later, Walter Hallstein, a former president of the EC Commission, put it succinctly when he stated, "We are not in business at all; we are in politics" (Ibid).

Another potential approach in achieving peace in Europe was to deal with defense matters directly. However, past attempts such as the European Political and Defence Communities—had already failed by 1956. Monnet and Schuman understood that, given the extent of mistrust after the war, the indirect approach of economic integration was the only one likely to be acceptable to all parties at the time.

Trade Promotes Peace

Increasing international trade might improve security in three related ways. First, more trade means greater economic interdependence between two countries. This increases the stake each country has in the welfare of its neighbor, and makes war more costly. It also increases the number of people who have an economic interest in peaceable relations and so helps to increase the political pressure against war making.

Second, more trade means more interaction between the peoples and governments of the two countries, more familiarity with the neighbor's goods and services, and greater familiarity with their cultural, political and social institutions. All of these are likely to raise trust.

Third, secure trading relations reduce the likelihood of war by increasing security of access to the partner's supplies of strategic raw materials and reducing the threat of trade embargo. This concern is especially important in a world of high trade barriers where access to other sources is more difficult. This was the situation in Europe around 1950 when Monnet and other French leaders were concerned that the German coal barons in the Ruhr would have too much control over French industry (Duchene, 1994). As the post-World War I solution of direct control of German resources had been discredited and was not an option, Monnet pushed for the creation of the European Community of Steel and Coal (ECSC) whereby Germany could rebuild its industry without being a threat to France. This sectoral approach to security was later expanded to the integration of general trade relations with the creation of the European Economic Community (EEC).

Economists have examined some of the implications of uncertain access to strategic raw materials. Arad and Hillman (1979) show how a fear of being cut off from foreign sources of defense equipment can cause countries to over-invest in their own defense industries. Similarly, Hillman and Long (1983) consider the optimal exploitation of a mineral resource if the alternative foreign supply was uncertain. In both these cases, regional bloc or a global institution that assured partner supplies would be both politically and economically advantageous.

A fourth possible strategic benefit of trade is that the greater trust generated by increased trade may, in time, pay a peace dividend as defence spending falls. Moreover, in all these cases one can envisage a virtuous circle whereby increasing trade permits closer integration, first through more thorough trade liberalization and then through policy or deep integration, each step of which binds the parties closer together and facilitates yet further growth in trade.

Although direct evidence of trade's impact on the likelihood of conflict between any pair of countries is limited, a large number of studies have confirmed the 1984 works of David Chan that conflict is less prevalent between countries if *both* are democratic (Chan, 1984). Philips Polachek (1992) explains this finding through the effect of democracy on international trade (Polachek, 1992). He estimates that democracies trade more with each other than other countries, and – using detailed data from the Conflict and Peace Data Bank – finds trade to have a significant and negative impact on conflict. He estimates that a 6% increase in trade lowers his measure of conflict by about 1% (Ibid). A key feature of his results is that Polachek tested for causality in this connection: he found that an increase in trade between partners caused a reduction in conflict but not the opposite (Ibid).

None of this subsection argues that trade does not always promote peace, nor that trade is sufficient for peace. Quite clearly trade partners do fight and sometimes over trade issues but on the whole it is persuasive that trade will generally tend to foster peaceable if not friendly relations between countries.

How Does Regional Bloc Promotes Peace?

The previous subsection concerned trade in general, implicitly, non-discriminatory trade but it is widely held that discriminatory trade has the same effect. This seems highly plausible under certain conditions, but, as we see below, it is not always the case.

Comparative political scientists have researched the use of trade diplomacy within a regional context, and concluded that trade relations, including regional economic communities, and especially deeper arrangements, might assist political relations between member countries by developing means for intra-mural conflict avoidance and management. The negotiations between leaders of neighboring countries that are required to form and operate a regional economic community tend to generate trust between themselves. This helps them to identify with each other, understand each other's problems and interpret each other actions. Trade talks allow political and/or economic elites to form coalitions for subsequent collaboration and consensual action. Wellerstin Wallace (1994) argues that the "most striking phenomenon of formal European integration has been the interpenetration of national administrations, with ministers and officials from different governments in close and continuous contact" (Wallace, 1994).

The main motivation for creating the ECSC in 1951, and the European Economic Community in 1957, was to reduce the threat of war in Europe, especially between France and Germany. Similar motives are found in the creation of ASEAN (to reduce tensions between Indonesia and Malaysia; De Rosa in 1995), APEC and CACM, which include potential political/military opponents in the same year (Page, 1998). Anwar (1994) views ASEAN's role as promoter of regional peace, with intra-regional conflicts among the five founding members before ASEAN was founded, but not afterwards. Andrea Srinivasan (1994) argues that greater economic interdependence amongst South Asian countries would help defuse tensions amongst them (Srinivasan, 1994). He states, "promoting freer movement of goods, services, people and capital in the region might also facilitate the resolution of political and territorial disputes" (Ibid).

Security also seems to have played an important role in the southern cone. The Argentine and Brazilian militaries long claimed resources were based in part on potential threats from each other. The countries signed nuclear cooperation and economic agreements (covering steel and automobiles) in the mid 1980s with the expectation that this would help reduce tensions between them by curtailing the power of the military and strengthening their fragile democracies. The creation of MERCOSUR in 1991 reinforced this process and bound smaller neighbors into it.

Rubens Ricupero, former Secretary General of UNCTAD and former finance minister in the Brazilian government, confirmed the importance of Mercosur's security aspects. Both countries were emerging from a period of military governments, during which considerable tension had characterized the bilateral relationship, centered on a long-standing controversy about competing hydro-electric projects in the international rivers of the Plata Basin. Both militaries had also continued to pursue their secret nuclear programs. It was essential to start with agreements in the economic areas in order to create a more positive external environment that rendered it possible to contain the military nuclear programs, and to replace rivalry by integration. This effort was developed along successive stages and eventually led to signature by the two governments of Brazil and Argentina" (private communication, 1998). Thus, as with the ECSC and European Community, the indirect path to enhancing security provided by economic integration was deemed an essential first step.

There is also a related example from Africa. In 2020, all the 16 members of the Economic Community of Western African States (ECOWAS) ratified a mutual defense protocol. This authorizes military intervention by the community in conflicts between members or if conflict in a member country is instigated from outside and is likely to endanger peace and security in the entire community. Former President of Gambia Yahya Jammeh relinquished power to Adama Barrow on 21st January 2017 after the intervention by the ECOWAS standby force. One interpretation of this; creating institutions that span beyond a leader's control and undertake military interventions without fear is almost unique achievement in the West Africa, ECOWAS region. Also social and economic achievement allowed neighbors to develop cooperative behaviors that eventually enhanced them to address mutual security concerns. In fact, under this view, ECOWAS has gone further than either Mercosur and the EU, for it uses an actual defense pact to bolster security while the others use only economic integration.

In cases where security is an issue and is amenable to trade-related policy, it can be shown that creating regional blocs could be the optimal approach. Under such circumstances we can also infer that the optimal level of protection that regional economic bloc-members maintain against imports from non-members will fall through time as trade grows and also following regional integration policy. This last observation serves two possible purposes: first, as a test for identifying countries' unobservable motivations for creating an regional economic bloc: if security were the main motive, tariffs would fall; hence if tariffs do not fall, regardless of the rhetoric behind creation, we know that the efficient pursuit of security was not its main objective. Second, the observation serves as a policy prescription for 'security-inspired' regional economic bloc.

Regional Integration: Modeling Trade and Security Externalities

If increased trade between two countries reduces tensions between them because of increased trust and economic dependency, what can economists say about the type of intervention that can capture this security externality? Schiff and Winters (1998) examines this issue within a formal three-country model, with two small antagonistic countries and a large "rest of the world". The model shows that, absent security externalities, non-discriminatory free trade is the optimal policy for the two small countries. But, if increased mutual imports provide additional security for small countries, it is worth subsidizing them by lowering their price relative to other goods. This could be done directly, but given the fiscal objections to subsidies, and their liability to capture, it is more frequently done by creating a regional economic bloc that taxes imports from the rest of the world, raises their price and therefore lowers the relative price of intra-bloc imports. The arrangement is optimal and (welfare is maximized) when external tariffs are set so that the marginal benefit from security-including a "peace dividend" from reduced defense expenditures - equals the marginal costing for trade diversion. Under these circumstances, the net welfare impact of forming regional economic bloc is positive and not ambiguous, as it would be in the absence of security effects.

Strictly speaking, to be equivalent to an import subsidy, the regional economic bloc should be accompanied by taxes on domestic sales to raise their price relative to member imports also, but even if this is not done, there will be security benefits from the trade preferences (though the optimal tariffs in this case are lower). The case for a regional economic bloc is strengthened if security is related to both imports from and exports to the potentially antagonistic partner and there may be yet further benefits because in this case full optimization requires countries to co-operate.

Over time, the optimal tariff on imports from nonmembers is likely to fall in such a security-inspired regional economic bloc. As antagonism between the two countries diminishes due to increased intra-bloc trade, the subsidy on intra-bloc trade (or the optimal external tariff) falls. Thus, if security is the main motivation for forming the regional economic community, the regional economic bloc's external trade policy should become increasingly open over time. This is precisely what took place in the EU: average tariffs on manufacturing products fell from about 13% in 1958 to about 3% after the Uruguay joined the trade.

Are trade preferences the only way to obtain security benefits? Since deep integration can also lower trading costs and increase trade flows, they can also add security even in the absence of trade preferences (and if external trade barriers are present, their optimal level falls following deep integration). But it seems likely that countries will engage in deep integration—which implies giving up a degree of sovereignty — only with countries they already trust. If trust is initially low, trade preferences may be the only available instrument until the degree of trust has increased. This, in fact, increases the warranted level of the external tariff in the early stages of an RTAs, for preferences not only boost trade directly, but by creating conditions for deep integration in the future promising further security and economic gains later.

Are Regional Integrations Always Effective Routes to Peace?

In the EU and Mercosur, integration helped to enhance security by internalizing security externalities associated with intra-bloc trade. The main reason for their success in achieving this goal is that the members were actually looking for arrangements to solve a security problem, not an economic one, and that defense pacts were not feasible given low trust at the time. Thus, the objectives of these RTAs were political rather than economic, and member countries structured the RTAs in such a way as to attain those objectives. Among other things, economic gains and losses were shared in ways that were perceived as being fair by member countries. On the other hand, many other RTAs are motivated by economics. In these cases, an asymmetric distribution of their benefits and costs may result in frictions among member countries. In other words, the pursuit of economic gain may result in security losses if the gains for one member come essentially at the expense of other members.

Thus, the result that trade enhances security does not allow us to conclude that policies which promote trade within a region will always improve the prospects of regional peace. Indeed, they may have precisely the opposite effect. This is because policy-induced integration promotes trade at a price. The tariff preferences, which induce regional trade, can create powerful income transfers within the region and can lead to the concentration of industry in a single location. The countries or regions, which lose income or industry, can be sufficiently resentful that separatist movements arise and the overall risk of conflict is increased. In such cases, disintegration may be the appropriate policy - e.g. East and West Pakistan.

A clear example of how integration can trigger conflict was the American Civil War. The northern states produced goods, which were sold to the southern states, and the southern states produced cotton, which was exported to Europe. A civil war was nearly triggered by these tariffs in 1828. The United States was already a customs union, but in that year Congress, dominated by northern interests, sharply raised the US import duty on goods. The effect of this was to increase the price which northern manufacturers could charge in the South, and so generated a massive income transfer from the South to the North. The policy was referred to in the South as the 'Tariff of Abominations'. South Carolina refused to collect it and threatened to secede unless it was rescinded. The Federal government sent in troops but Congress backed down before fighting developed. In 1860 northern interests tried again, and this time Congress would not back down. This, perhaps as much as slavery, was the issue, which led the southern states to try to quit the Union, and led to the bloodiest conflict of the nineteenth century (Adams, 1993). Of course, the USA was deeply and politically integrated by this time, so that a less violent 'divorce' was probably impossible to achieve. However, the potential divisiveness of trade preferences is plain in the example.

A second example is the East African Common Market. In this case Kenya was the equivalent of the northern states of America. Tanzania and Uganda complained about the income transfers, which the common external tariff on goods created. They also feared that there would be an increasing agglomeration of manufacturing in Nairobi, which had a head start on industrialization compared with the smaller industrial centers of Tanzania at Dar es Salaam and Uganda at Jinja. Arguments about compensation for the income transfers led to the collapse of the Common Market, the closing of borders, and the confiscation of Community assets in 1978. In turn, this atmosphere of hostility contributed to conflict between Tanzania and Uganda in 1979.

In these examples the trade policy used to promote regional integration was so unfair that it actually worsened intra-regional security. In this light, the success of the EU looks even more remarkable. In addition to the genuine desire for security noted above (due perhaps to Europe's extraordinarily bloody history – three Franco-German conflicts in a century – and the failure of a number of alternative efforts at integration – e.g. the European Political and Defence Communities). France and Germany, the key players in the EEC, were relatively evenly balanced. Had they not been, an alternative solution to the security problem – hegemonic domination – would have been more likely than the reliance on mutual benefits that characterizes the RTA route.

Second, in reflection of the genuine wish for reconciliation, the European Community has always pursued regional integration in ways that avoid transfers large enough to trigger conflict. This was partly as a matter of negotiating style and partly as detailed design (Winters, 1997). The style was consensual: negotiators were always looking for compromise and conciliation. When a country signaled that a Community policy would cause it major political or economic problems it was accommodated, either by being offered compensation, as with the British budget rebate negotiated by Prime Minister Thatcher, or by being granted a very gradual adjustment process, as with compliance with the rules on labor mobility by Spain and Portugal. The key design feature was that the Community's external tariffs were generally low and declining. Hence, the income transfers arising from producers in one nation-exploiting consumers in another were relatively small.

The one exception to this was agriculture: it has been very highly protected and has generated large income transfers between countries; it has also been a source of some internal political conflict. In grand terms, however, even agriculture was part of the inspired peace-bargain. The policy arose because France wanted access to German markets at the high prices which German farmers also desired. The conflict over agriculture has not often been Franco-German, but rather between them and other members, especially the British.

The economic costs of forming security-enhancing RTAs are important, even if the objective is as apparently non-economic as securing peace. Before deciding whether to form such an RTA, it behooves policy makers to convince themselves that trade will enhance trust significantly – that contact will help not harm general relations and that it will create no new frictions. These countries should also ask whether an RTA is the most efficient mechanism to internalize them. Should they choose to form and RTA for security reasons, policy makers should ensure that tariffs are not set higher than is absolutely necessary to capture the security externalities that exist, and realize that these tariffs should decline over time and following deeper measures of integration.

Regional Integration and Migration

The formation of an RTA is sometimes seen as a means of preventing or reducing the spread of civil disturbances or civil war from neighboring nations – or of controlling the migratory flows they induce. The EU has been concerned with such threats in North Africa and this has been one motivation behind the Euro-Med Agreements between these Mediterranean countries and the EU. The hope is that these agreements, including their associated aid protocols will improve the economic situation in those countries and help contain these problems. Similarly, both the US and Mexico have been concerned with the possibility of occasional social strife and violence in Mexico spreading northwards, and both hoped that NAFTA, by improving access to US markets, would help to improve Mexico's economic situation and reduce social tensions. Implicit in this hope is that NAFTA increases Mexican economic welfare.

Closely related is the manifest desire of rich countries to stem large-scale migration from poorer countries even if it does not immediately threaten political and social stability. This too has played a role in the formation of RTAs. It applies to the EC in its Europe Agreements with the CEECs, and to the US in NAFTA (OECD, 1995). Presidents Salinas and Bush argued that by helping Mexico to export more goods NAFTA would help it to export fewer people, thereby reducing the migration pressure. And the recent Euro-Med agreements also provide examples of such motivation.

However, whether RTAs do help to resolve migration problems depends on whether trade and migration are complements or substitutes. Standard trade theory holds that they are substitutes, so that increased trade integration is likely to reduce income or wage differentials and lower labor migration flows. More recent analysis, however, and some empirical results have concluded that North-South trade and migration may well be complementary, so that integration may not lower migration, especially that of unskilled labor.

Four main arguments lead in this direction. First, one may plausibly argue that migration entails a fixed cost and that developing country capital markets are highly imperfect (Lopez and Schiff, 1998). If so, very poor people may not be able to afford migration and a policy that increased their income could relax their capital constraint and allow th whichem to move. Second, the costs of migration decrease as more information about the destination country becomes available. Since, for the reasons discussed above, this seems likely for an RTA, migration to the new members could increase.

Third, even if an RTA is welfare improving overall – which, it has been argued and one cannot take for granted – it may not benefit the unskilled workers, who are the real *bête noire* of the potential countries of immigration. For example, since the mid-1980s, unskilled workers have fared poorly in Mexico, with declines in real income of 10-15% to the extent that this is a result of NAFTA (Hanson and Harrison, 1999). The incentives for these people, if not their ability, to emigrate are increased by integration. Finally, the changes in the production structure induced by an RTA will cause some people to migrate internally within member countries. Evidence suggests that once they have been shaken loose from their 'homeland', peoples' propensities to migrate internationally increase. That is, having once uprooted and, say, moved from rural areas to Mexico City or to the US borderlands, it is a small additional step to move further to the USA itself (Sewastynowicz, 1986, Morrison & Zabin, 1994).

Migration remains an issue even within Common Markets in which free mobility of labour is ostensibly an objective. Thus the EU required Portugal and Spain to wait through a thirteen-year transition period before being permitted completely free access to other members' labour markets. Similarly, it is widely accepted that a fear of migration is one of the reasons behind the long reluctance of the EU to consider Turkish membership seriously. Even among long-standing members of the EU, migration has not been made easy, and labour mobility is much lower in Europe than in the USA (Blanchard and Katz, 1992). In part this is cultural, but in part it reflects a whole series of policy frictions, such as pension transferability, housing systems and health provision, that make effective migration complicated or worse.

Regional Integration: Democracy and Political Institutions

RTAs can also be useful tools to improve political institutions. Trade blocs with strong "club rules" can help anchor democratic reforms in member countries. Membership in an RTA can increase the likelihood of achieving or upholding democracy, especially if the bloc includes large and developed democratic countries. Newer or less politically developed countries may gain from joining an RTA that includes a large developed country or countries if accession is part of a strategy to pursue political, economic or social reforms (or prevent backsliding) that would not be feasible without the conditionality embodied in the REC's "club rules." Those rules often include democracy and human rights.

Mercosur put its – then informal – democracy rule into practice in April 1996 when the commander of Paraguay's armed forces was said to be contemplating a military coup. The bloc's four presidents (with backing from the United States and the Organization of American States) reportedly quelled the rumored coup with a strong joint statement that democracy was a condition of membership in the bloc. Two months later Mercosur amended its charter to formally exclude any country that "abandons the full exercise of republican institutions" (Presidential Declaration on the Democratic Commitment in Mercosur, San Luis, Argentina, June 25, 1996; Talbott, 1996; Survey on MERCOSUR, The Economist, October 12, 1996). In forming RTAs with Mercosur, Chile and Bolivia accepted democracy as a condition for membership (Protocol of Ushuaia, July 24, 1998).

The EEC had no formal democracy requirement, although by convention and practice it was understood from the mid-1960s that such a condition existed, at least for new members. Bhalla and Bhalla (1997) argue that it was generally understood that "the acceptance of the poorer economies of Greece, Spain and Portugal was motivated largely by the desire to help these restored democracies remain democratic by bolstering them politically and economically". Similarly, the Europe Agreements with accession candidates in Central and Eastern Europe and the Baltics are designed to "facilitate" their "full integration into the community of democratic nations" (Title 1, Article 2). Latvia, one of the candidates for EU accession, is reviewing its citizenship policies for its Russian minority to meet EU concerns about human rights (Washington Post, 7/24/1998). The EU agreements with Mediterranean countries also include respect for human rights and the rule of law, as does the Contonou Agreement between the EU and the ACP countries. In the 1992 Treaty on European Union, explicit reference was made to democracy, although not in any operational form.

Conditions for democracy and human rights will be truly effective only if the penalties for violating them are severe and their enforcement credible. As with the credibility of economic policies as discussed earlier, it is difficult to pin down exactly what inspires credibility, but for developing countries an explicit statement of the club rule seems necessary, and an explicit and plausible plan for its enforcement is highly desirable. In the absence of such conditions it is difficult to see how the result will be achieved, and, in particular, how it will be achieved without the need to resort to the sort of explicit political pressure accordingly.

The enforceability of such club rules depends on both the value of belonging to the bloc and the credibility of the threat of action. Regarding the value of belonging to the bloc, new members who obtain significant benefits when joining a large bloc, including access to a large market and greater bargaining power with the rest of the world, are unlikely to break the rules (or backslide) and risk losing the benefits of membership. It is true that parties threatening democracy may not be moved by such considerations, but ordinary economic agents will be and so the condition will make it more difficult to build support for insurrection. Second, the credibility of the threat of action is likely to be greater if breaking club rules by new members entail a large cost to the other members. That cost maybe direct and economic or perhaps more likely, indirect and political, such as a domino effect.

The effectiveness of such "democracy only" rules is likely to vary with the nature of the membership. RECs between small low-income countries, which typically trade very little with each other, are less able to impose major costs on recalcitrant by ejecting them. Hence choosing large (important) partners improves the chances of club rules being enforced. Because a country is likely to be more concerned with a nearby than with a distant country's social and political institutions, enforcement of club rules is also likely to be more effective in RECs between neighbors than one between distant partners.

Two other conditions will affect the credibility of enforcement. First, it seems unlikely that non-democracies, or even countries where democracy is very fragile, will prove stern disciplinarians even if a democratic rule exists. Second, the enforcer has to see enforcement as an important issue for itself. We have noted the importance of proximity in this, and it is also important that there be no other issues of greater importance. While the Cold War was in progress, western powers were far more concerned to ensure that client countries were securely anti-communist than with the details of their governance structures. Thus imposing democratic rules was just not an element of policy.

The question of distance is relevant to one current debate. The EU's Contonou Agreement with the ACP states intends eventually to replace the Lomé Convention by a series of Regional Economic Partnership Agreements (REPAs) with groups of ACP countries (McQueen, 1998). It includes an 'essential element', the developing partners' respect for human rights and democracy, as well as injunctions to manage their economies properly (Council of the European Union, 1998). Some commentators (Winters, 2001) argue that the EU's interest in enforcing good economic policy on the ACP countries, let alone 'good' political practice, is very doubtful. The ACP countries are too small and distant to affect any EU interest materially and different EU members frequently feel differently about any particular case. However, ACP trade with EU has increased to fifty percent in July 2022. In addition, disciplining former colonies for pursuing economic or political policies that are not approved in European capitals looks like an international public relations nightmare. On this view, REPAs will generate no additional credibility for the ACP countries.

A contrary view — at least on economic credibility — is given by Paul Collier et al (1997). They see the EU as the stern external agent of restraint that developing countries require in order to convince the world that they are reliable and will succeed economically (Collier et al, 1997). Their argument is essentially that the EU is so important to the ACP countries, that they would never flout it, so that the EU can do a little good to its partners at almost no cost to itself.

One of the interesting features of the club-rules/democracy argument for RECs is that it is one case where there is clearly no multilateral substitute. Multilateral trade arrangements cannot propose and enforce these sorts of rules, because they are simply not part of the mandate of organizations such as the WTO. Other international organizations, such as the UN or regional and multilateral development institutions may be able to convince member countries to abide by some rules, but so far, these rules do not include democracy or other constraints on political regimes. It would appear that positive spillover effects in the political arena are only possible in large regional arrangements that include club rules.

Regional Integration and Strengthening of Nation State

Joining an REC necessarily requires surrendering some immediate control over policy making and losing some political autonomy, if only over tariffs on partners' exports (so, of course, does membership of the WTO.) Some RECs, however, go deeper than this and create institutions for joint decision-making. For example, as the European Union's integration has deepened, decision-making has increasingly moved away from national capitals to Brussels, and much of the current debate is shaped by the belief that some form of political unification must eventually follow the creation of an integrated economic unit. But such integration need not result in the suppression of the nation as an organizational framework or the loss of effective sovereignty. On the contrary, by pooling sovereignty, members of RECs may be able to preserve and enlarge it, and thus strengthen the concept of national identity and integrity. Nation states can strengthen themselves by creating a united front against external forces, or by joining forces in international negotiations. Setting aside considerations of coalition-building and policy spillovers.

Regional Integration, Outside Threats and Regional Hegemons

The normal approach to external security threats is for countries to form alliances independently of any trade preferences. However, it is possible to start with a trade pact, based on "hopes that economic union between the weak would ripen into political union, and that by the political union of the weak a power might be established strong enough to defend against aggression from outside" (Viner, 1950). Nations that feared being absorbed through coercion by larger states have united to forestall such coercion.

Thus, an Austrian emperor proposed (but eventually aborted) an economic union with Spain and Bavaria as a defensive scheme against France in 1665 (Ibid). Moreover, the Gulf Cooperation Council (GCC) was created in 1981 partly in response to the potential threat of regional powers such as Iran and Iraq (Schiff and Winters, 1998), and ASEAN was partially motivated by a perceived need to stem the threat of spreading communism in the region. A major motive of Central and Eastern European countries in applying for membership to the EU was as protection against a perceived threat from Russia.

The Southern African Development Coordination Conference (SADCC) also falls into this class. It was initially formed in 1980 to provide a united front against, and reduce dependence on, South Africa. After Apartheid ended South Africa was invited to join the group, now the Southern African Development Community (SADC). The difference was that, while SADCC entailed cooperation on trade matters in general, it did not involve mutual trade preferences *per se*. SADC, on the other hand, perhaps because it lacks the outside threat has developed a trade protocol based on preferences.

Regional Integration and Negotiations with the Outside World

Regional cooperation (which can, but need not, involve trade preferences) can strengthen the voices of small nations, which often face severe disadvantages in dealing with the rest of the world due to low bargaining power and high negotiation costs. Bilateral and multilateral negotiations often require substantial financial resources, time, and expert knowledge, which are limited in small countries. As the world has become more integrated and the number of issues to be dealt with in the international arena has grown, the incentive for small countries to co-operate with their neighbors has grown as well.

Small countries can substantially reduce their negotiation costs and, at the same time, increase their market and negotiation power, by pooling their negotiation resources and by acting together to articulate shared interests. This is more likely to come about (Schiff, 1998):

- If their interests are similar (so that intra-bloc negotiation costs are low);
- If the cost of international negotiations is high (greater incentives to co-operate); and
- If a large number of issues need to be dealt with (which both increases the incentives and makes it easier to construct packages in which every party can gain).

Establishing a regional grouping typically involves "logrolling".

This is described by Michael Schiff (1998) as he argues "I'll vote for your issue if you vote for mine"; by trading support for each other's preferred issues, countries can get more than they could obtain unilaterally (Schiff, 1998). However, it is well to be aware that even with logrolling such coalition-formation is neither easy nor common. Members will usually have to sacrifice some preferred positions even before the international negotiation process begins as the coalition settles priorities. These steps can be politically difficult, especially if the group is large and the countries differ widely. The coalition also needs to devise ways of responding to offers and set-backs in negotiations, for it is quite certain that they will not achieve all that they hope for initially. Setting up a secretariat and devising suitable institutional rules for decision-taking may help in these processes, but this requires significant time and resources up front. Relatively shallow but highly successful examples of co-operation of this kind are the Scandinavian and ASEAN groups in the WTO. These blocs pool their resources to attend meetings, providing regular briefings for each other. If they agree on an issue (and they put some effort into discovering before-hand whether they do or not), the representatives may speak for the group, but if not, individual countries look after their own interests. At a deeper level, small Caribbean nations increased their bargaining power by establishing the Caribbean Community (CARICOM) in 1973 to pool their negotiation resources and formulate common policy stances. This allowed the member states to lower negotiation costs and have greater influence outside of the region than would have been possible if they had acted independently. The region acquired bargaining power at the very highest level of North-South politics. Representatives of CARICOM countries took the lead in formulating and articulating the positions of the ACP Group in negotiating the Lomé Conventions. By pooling their support, the CARICOM nations succeeded in getting their nationals elected to key international positions such as Commonwealth Secretary General and ACP Secretary General. In the process, they ensured that the region's interests in commodity trade and development cooperation were taken into account. They also consolidated multilateral links with other parts of the developing world, and established themselves as full participants in the activities of the United Nations, despite that organization's earlier ambivalence on the issue of microstate member-ship. CARICOM countries focused on getting UN organs to address the development needs of Small Island developing states. Finally, they succeeded in collectively negotiating a whole range of preferential market access agreements (e.g., CARIBCAN with Canada, CBI with the US, and Lomé and (along with other developing nations) GSP with the EU). Despite its relatively limited trade and investment impact, CARICOM was successful in serving as a political instrument in joint negotiations on trade and investment with larger countries and regional trading blocs.

The existence of a visible regional and supranational authority may attract more foreign assistance (or even foreign direct investment), as it is easier for the donor community to deal with the group as an entity than with each country individually. William Inotai (1991) writes:

> *"More recently, common activities emerged in order to attract higher volumes of external financial resources. By 1988, SADCC ensured external financing for 20 industrial projects, and has now worked on getting additional resources for 11 more projects" (Inotai, 1991).*

And SADC - SADCC's successor - now acts as a regional coordinat-ing mechanism with the donor community. For instance, in February 1996, the US Department of Commerce signed a memorandum of understanding with SADC that outlines six areas for cooperation in advancing commercial development in Southern Africa.

As for other RTAs, Japanese aid has played a major role in assisting regional industrial projects in ASEAN, such as automobile assembly and parts production (Bhalla and Bhalla, 1997). Similarly, following its vocation for regionalism as a principle, the European Union has actively assisted sub-regional integration – for example, in Central Europe and the Mediterranean.

Finally, the objective of strengthening negotiating and bargaining power is not limited to the formation of blocs by small countries. James Whalley (1998) argues that the countries involved in the creation of the EEC in the late 1950s felt that individually they might have limited leverage in a negotiation with the US, but together they would have much greater leverage. And similar arguments were made in Britain when she joined the EEC (Whalley, 1998). Similarly, Whalley (1998) further argues that the objective of increasing negotiating power has also been present in the formation of Mercosur, especially vis-a-vis NAFTA (Ibid). The issue of market power, however, as opposed to negotiating efficiency, considers the effects of regional integration on the process of global trade liberalization.

Gains/Benefits of Regional Integration

The gains are divided into traditional and non-traditional.

Traditional gains
a) Trade gains
- If goods are sufficiently strong substitutes, Regional Trade Agreements (RTAs) will cause the demand for third party goods to decrease, which will drive down prices.
- Acute competition in the trade zone may induce outside firms to cut prices to maintain exports to the region.
- The risk of trade diversion – low external tariffs 'open regionalism.

b) Increased returns and increased competition

- Within a tiny market, there may be a trade-off between economies of scale and competition, and market enlargement removes this trade-off and makes possible the existence of:

  i. Large firms with greater productive efficiency for any industry with economies of scale; and

  ii. Increased competition that induces firms to cut prices, expand sales and reduce internal inefficiencies

- Countries with the most cost effective infrastructure and human resources (i.e. head-start countries) would be the beneficiaries.

c) Investment

- RTAs may attract Foreign Direct Investment (FDI), both from within and outside the region as a result of:

- Market enlargement (particularly for 'lumpy' investment that might only be viable above a certain size, and

- Production rationalization (reduced distortion and lower marginal cost in production).

- Enlarging a sub-regional market will bring FDI, which will be beneficial, provided that the incentive for foreign investors is not to engage in 'tariff-jumping' - requires reduced protection, specifically external tariffs.

Non-traditional Gains

a) Lock in to domestic reforms

- Enables government to pursue policies that are welfare improving but time inconsistent in the absence of the RTAs (e.g. adjustment of tariffs in the face of terms of trade shocks, confiscation of foreign investment, etc.,- RTA acts as commitment mechanism, especially for trade policy.

b) Signaling

- Despite the cost (e.g. investment in political capital and transaction costs) – enables a country to signal its policy orientation/approach, or some underlying conditions of the economy (competitiveness of the industry, sustainability of the exchange rate) in order to attract investment.

c) Insurance

- RTAs provide insurance to its members against future hazards (macroeconomic instability, terms of trade shocks, trade war, resurgence of protectionism in developed countries, etc.) (e.g. with asymmetric terms-of-trade shocks (such as with oil in Nigeria and the rest of ECOWAS), "insurance" may become an important rationale for integration.

d) Coordination and bargaining power

- Coordination made easier than through multilateral agreements since negotiation rules accustom countries to a give-and-take approach trade-offs between different policy areas possible - collective bargaining power is relevant for the poor and fractioned countries within a sub-region – countries develop a common position and bargain as a group (increased visibility, credibility and better negotiation outcomes).

e) Security

- Increase inter-regional trade and investment and links countries in a web of positive interactions and interdependency.
- Build trust, raise the cost of war, and hence reduce the risk of conflicts between countries.
- Improves intra-regional security through the development of a culture of cooperation and mechanisms to address issues of common interest – cooperation may extend to "common defense" or mutual military assistance, hence increasing global security.

CHAPTER FOUR

Current Status of East African Community

As indicated in the introduction, the East African Community is a regional block of seven states comprising of Republic of Kenya, Republic of Uganda, United Republic of Tanzania, Republic of Rwanda, Republic of Burundi, Republic of South Sudan and Democratic Republic of Congo. The EAC was founded in 1967, collapsed in 1977 and revived in 1999 by the Republic of Kenya, Republic of Uganda and the United Republic of Tanzania.

The Republic of South Sudan acceded to the EAC Treaty on 15th April 2016 and it deposited the instruments of Accession in a colourful ceremony held in Dar es Salaam on 6th October 2016 in the Submit of the Heads of States and Governments. President Salva Kiir Mayardit of the Republic of South Sudan deposited the instruments of Accession to the EAC Secretariat Organ in Arusha, Tanzania. The nascent state was given three years stay of application till October 2019 to implement all the protocols of the Community beginning with a customs union, common market and monetary union. However, South Sudan has been quite slow in implementing these three protocols.

Democratic Republic of Congo Accession to the East African Community

In 2010, Tanzanian officials expressed interest in inviting the Democratic Republic of Congo to join the East African Community. The DRC had applied for admission to the EAC in June 2019. The interest of Tanzania is for the DRC to give the EAC Partner States its first port on the African West coast. In June 2021, the EAC Summit launched a verification mission to assess the suitability of the DRC for admission to the Community, and has since drafted a report on their findings, which was submitted to the EAC Council of Ministers. On 23 November 2021; Ministers in charge of East African Community (EAC) Affairs recommended for consideration by the EAC Heads of States the report of the verification team on the application by The Democratic Republic of Congo (DRC) to join the Community. In February 2022, the EAC Council of Ministers recommended that the DRC be admitted as a new member state of the EAC. On 18 March 2022, the EAC Secretary General Dr. Peter Mathuki confirmed that the Heads of States would approve the admission on 29 March 2022. The Democratic Republic of the Congo became a member of the EAC on 29th March 2022, at a virtual Head of State summit chaired by Uhuru Kenyatta, President of the Republic of Kenya. It was an important decision for Congolese all over the world and as they celebrated the admission of their troubled country to the regional block. The admission to the EAC is guided by some criteria as stipulated in the Treaty.

Criteria for Accession to the EAC as provided by the Treaty (Article 3)

a. Acceptance of the Community as set out in this Treaty;
b. Adherence to universally acceptable principles of good governance, democracy, the rule of law, observance of human rights

and social justice;

c. Potential contribution to the strengthening of integration within the East African region;

d. Geographical proximity to and inter-dependence between it and the Partner States;

e. Establishment and maintenance of a market driven economy; and

f. Social and economic policies being compatible with those of the Community.

However, the above six criteria have not been met by all the Partner States even the amongst founders and traditional members of the community. This therefore shows that the Community admission is politically motivated and not technically accessed against the six spelled out criteria by the Treaty.

EAC Achievements

I. Confidence building measures
   a. Treaty signed
   b. Protocols ratified
   c. MOUs on cooperation in defence signed
   d. Signing of MOU on foreign policy coordination

II. Harmonisation of policies
   a. Convertibility of currencies
   b. Reading of budget statements on the same day
   c. Implementation of preferential tariff discount
   d. Harmonisation of standards of goods and services as East African standards
   e. Mutual recognition of health certificates issued by partner states

III. Easing of cross border movement of persons and goods
   a. East African passports
   b. Seven days' grace period for personal motor vehicles
   c. Immigration desks for East Africans at international airports
   d. Re-introduction of interstate passes
   e. Withdrawal of visa charges for students
   f. Monitoring mechanisms launched
   g. Tripartite framework with SADC, COMESA
      • EAC joint trade review by World Trade Organisation (WTO)
      • Negotiation of Economic Partnership Agreements (EPAs) as a bloc such as EAC-UK-EPA
      • Signed TIFA with USA as a bloc
      • Annual organization of Jua kali/Nguvu kazi (informal sector)
      • Tripartite Summit together with COMESA and SADC for single FTA
      • Formation of councils such as science commission, Kiswahili Commission etc.
      • Infrastructure development Athi river Namanga, Arusha road, various master plans
      • Peace and security programmes
      • Joint military operations and games
      • Health programmes and research
      • Customs union implementation
      • Development of instruments for common procedures, NTBs monitoring and elimination
      • Joint investment promotion in the region and abroad
      • Joint tourism promotion
      • Energy conferences
      • Petroleum conferences
      • Negotiations of various instruments

- Gender programs
- Education programs including student essays
- Communication programs, etc
- Productive and social programs such as industry, agriculture, animal husbandry, climate and environment
- Fast tracking federation programs
- EALA programmes
- Lake Victoria programs
- Court cases which have been executed
- Legal advises

Enlargement of the East African Community

The realization of a large regional economic bloc encompassing Burundi, Kenya, Rwanda, Tanzania, Uganda, South Sudan and DR Congo with a population of 312 million people, land area of 4.8 million sq. kilometres (1,857,292 sq mi) and combined Gross Domestic Product of $332.764 billion, bears great strategic and geopolitical significance and prospects of a renewed and reinvigorated East African Community. The following countries have great potential to join the East African Community:

Ethiopia
Kenyan President Uhuru Kenyatta, the reigning Chair of the East African Community by then proposed expanding the EAC to include Central, Southern and Northern African states, such as Ethiopia. The potential joining of Ethiopia into the EAC would bring the membership population to approximately 420 million. Speaking at the opening of the One Stop Border Post (OSBP) in Moyale in 2020, Prime Minister Abiy Ahmed of Ethiopia affirmed his commitment to regional integration saying that the east African people are one people and economic integration is a key goal for the region to achieve so as to unlock its potential.

Malawi

In 2010, Tanzanian officials expressed interest in inviting Malawi to join the EAC. Malawian Foreign Affairs Minister Etta Banda said, however, that there were no formal negotiations taking place concerning Malawian membership.

Somalia

Representatives of Somalia applied for membership in the EAC in March 2012. The EAC Heads of State considered the application in December 2012, which requested that the EAC Council work with Somalia to verify their application. In February 2015, the EAC again deliberated on the matter but deferred a decision as verification had not yet started nor had preparations with the government of Somalia been finalized. As of June 2019, Somalia's application has been frozen due to instability in the country. However, President Hassan Sheik Mohamud during the EAC Extraordinary Summit of the Heads of States on 21st July 2022 in Arusha-Tanzania where he was invited as an observer, appealed to the EAC Heads of States to fast track the admission of the Federal Republic of Somalia.

Sudan

Sudan applied to join the EAC in 2011, but its membership is strongly opposed by Tanzania and Uganda. They contended that because of the Sudan's lack of a direct border with the EAC at the time, its allegedly discriminatory actions toward Black Africans, its record of human rights violations, and its history of hostilities with both South Sudan and Uganda, it was ineligible to join. The Sudan's application was rejected by the EAC in December 2011.

Zambia

In 1960s Zambia had unsuccessfully applied to join the EAC 2010. In 2010, Tanzanian officials expressed interest in inviting Zambia in applying for membership the EAC. During a state visit to Kenya on 15th June 2022, President Hichilema of Zambia mentioned to the EAC Chairman President Kenyatta, that Zambia was interested in joining an East African Consortium for negotiating trade agreements in oil and agricultural sectors.

CHAPTER FIVE

Status of Implementation of EAC Protocols

With its motto of "deepening integration and widening cooperation," the regional integration process is at a high pitch at the moment as reflected by the encouraging progress of the East African Customs Union, establishment in 2010 of the Common Market, Monetary Union/Common Currency (East African Shilling) in November 2013 with its implementation in 2023. The negotiations for the East African Federation all underscore the serious determination of the East African leadership and citizens to construct a powerful and sustainable East African economic and political bloc.

However, Tanzania has been reluctant in the fast tracking of the political federation of the region, something that can be termed as fears in that its citizens could be out competed in the job market when the region is federated. Unlike the other countries where English is the official language, in Tanzania, Kiswahili is the official language. Additionally, Tanzania already belongs to the South Africa Development Organization (SADC) and this complicates the custom union duties charges. For instance, shall Tanzania be considered in the EAC custom union territory or in SADC custom union territory? On the other hand, Kenya, Uganda and Rwanda appear keen

Stages of EAC Integration

on fast-tracking the political integration of the region even with Tanzania dragging its feet. Burundi is a poor country stuck with French as the language of instructions in schools and government offices and moreover due to its poor economic condition, it is not able to pay it annual member fees and cannot benefit from integration programmes. South Sudan is a conflict-ridden country and it is yet to officially launch the custom union, which is the baby protocol for the integration in the EAC. It is equally a poor country, has never paid its annual membership to the regional bloc and it is yet to benefit from the regional integration programmes. Though it has begun the implementation of a custom union, it process is quite slow.

Reflections on Customs Union: The Baby Protocol of the EAC

The enthusiasm of the EAC to facilitate trade among its members is enshrined in Article 5 (2) of the Treaty establishing the East African Community, which states that the first stage of EAC integration will be the formation of a Customs Union, skipping the earlier stages of Preferential Trade Area and Free Trade Area. The EAC Customs Union Protocol came into force in January 2005. The Customs Union has four major elements: (1) the establishment of a Common External Tariff (CET); (2) the establishment of EAC Rules of Origin (RoO) criteria, including Certificates of Origin and Simplified Certificates of Origin; (3) the internal elimination of tariffs for goods meeting the EAC RoO criteria and (4) the elimination of Non Tariff Barriers (NTBs).

The primary objective of the Protocol establishing the Customs Union is to facilitate inter and intra-regional trade in goods. The Treaty establishing the East African Community first gave birth to the Customs Union Protocol and as in the subsequent stages of EAC integration, then came the establishment of a Common Market, then a Monetary Union and ultimately a Political Federation in the offing.

Status of Custom Union Protocol Implementation

The strides taken by the EAC to have a Customs Union Protocol in force and a Community Law – the Customs Management Act – made it attractive to other countries such Rwanda and Burundi to accede the Treaty in June 2007. The latter two countries became fully-fledged members of the EAC in July 2007, and started to implement the Customs Union in 2009. The region of Southern Sudan had shown its interest to join the EAC as early the year of 2009. Currently the EAC is recognized globally and representatives from various countries and international organizations have submitted their credentials to the Secretary General of the East African Community. There are other countries envying to join the regional bloc, as the Summit of EAC Heads of State and Government have said in their 2021 Communiqué. The region has increased both inter- and intra-regional trade, and has also witnessed an increase in intra-EAC Foreign Direct Investments (FDI) as well as in FDI from outside. The East African Legislative Assembly (EALA) has passed several community laws and the Council of Ministers has established various Sectoral Councils to oversee policy issues in the regional integration progress.

There is mutual recognition of standards marks across the region where the bureaus of standards have developed an EAC catalogue of Standards. In pursuit of facilitating trade the EAC has embarked on a mission to establish One Stop Border Posts that have already been articulated within the auspices of the Community Law. Finally, the EAC Council of Ministers has recently approved the 'EAC Customs Valuation Manual' – a document that provides guidelines on how to implement and uniformly interpret EAC Custom's valuation provisions within the Community and therefore helps overcome challenges in this respect.

Indeed, the Custom Union Protocol began as part of general trade. Article X, GATT 1994 provides for publication of trade-related laws, regulations, rules and agreements in a prompt and accessible manner; restraint from enforcing measures of general application prior to their publication; and administration of the above-mentioned laws, regulations, rulings and agreements in a uniform, impartial and reasonable manner. Accordingly, the administration of Customs functions in East African countries is governed through the East Africa Customs Management Act – EAC CMA (2004) established by Article 39 of the Protocol for Establishment of the East African Customs Union of 2005. In all EAC Partner States customs is not a standalone department; for instance in Tanzania Customs is integral part of the Tanzania Revenue Authority and is assigned with annual revenue collection target like other taxation departments. The East Africa Community Treaty signed in 1999 provides for; *inter alia*, the establishment of East Africa Customs Union as a transitional stage to, and an integral part of the Community. The EAC Customs Administration includes; communication of customs and trade information among Partner States for purpose of prevention, investigation and suppression of customs offences; and the operation of a harmonized information system to facilitate the sharing of customs and trade information. This includes trade facilitation; simplification, standardization and harmonization of trade information and documentation; harmonization of commodity description and coding system; prevention, investigation and suppression of customs offences; trade liberalization to eliminate all internal tariffs, establish common external tariffs and removal of non-tariff barriers; trade related aspects such as rules of origin, anti-dumping measures, subsidies, countervailing and safeguard measures; export promotion schemes; special economic zones-free ports for the purpose of facilitating and promoting international trade and accelerating development within the Union; and exemption regime. The implementation of the Customs Union has enabled economic growth in the Community through elimination of internal tariffs, elimination of all trade barrier, adopting common external tariff, implementation of customs reforms and modernization initiatives, and removal of charges of equivalent effect. As a result intra EAC trade has grown significantly. Exports to the region grew at an annual average of 16% between 2005 and 2007 while imports grew an annual average of 11.2% during the same period. Foreign direct flows into the region have almost tripled from 692 million U.S dollars in 2002 to 1,763 million U.S. dollars in 2007 (Mugisa et al, 2009). The application of the Common External Tariff (CET) in the Union has resulted into positive impact on trade and growth in the region; increased liberalization as average applied tariffs have come down in all Partner States, enhanced predictability for exporters and investors and an increase in imports. Although divergent effects have been observed including reduced tariff for Kenya while Uganda and Tanzania has led to increased tariffs, and increases in tariffs dispersions from one product to another, across products within sectors, and across stages of production.

Common External Tariffs (CETs)

While the old CET rates were 0% for raw materials, 10% for intermediate goods and 25% for finished goods, the new CET rates are being proposed are 0% for raw materials, 10% for intermediate goods, 25% for finished goods and 35% for goods manufactured in sufficient quantities in EAC. The 4th tariff band is the 35%, which is being introduced for the first time.

According to the available data from the EAC Secretariat, this new tariff band, if implemented, will create an intra-EAC market value of 2.13 trillion shillings. Uganda, Kenya's biggest trading partner in the region is set to have the largest increase in market share valued at 967.9 million shillings with Kenya coming in second with an additional regional trade value of 583.7 million shillings. Rwanda will have the potential to increase the value of its exports in the region by at least 425.1 million shillings, Burundi 156.1 million shillings and Tanzania 33.3 million shillings. Locally produced goods and sectors protected by the CET include textiles, iron, and steel, automotive, agro-processing, wood, mineral processing, energy, fertilisers, and pharmaceuticals. The move is also expected to attract new investments into the region's industrial sector by having firms set up base within the EAC, particularly on processing secondary intermediates into finished products. The 4th band was expected to enter into force by 1st of July 2022.

EAC Stay of Application of the Common External Tariffs (CETs) under the Customs Union

It can be done under the following two conditions:
- EAC Partner States may request for a Stay of Application of the CET on Sensitive Products.
- Products brought into the EAC region under this arrangement will attract full CET when exported to another Partner State.

EAC Duty Remission Scheme under the Customs Union

EAC Duty Remission Schemes are offered in EAC as incentives for the infant industries to import raw materials and industrial inputs for the manufacture of exports. The products of the companies enjoying this facility are not eligible for EAC Community Tariff Preferences when traded within the EAC.

Although the intra-EAC trade still stands at 15%, the region boasts for 16 billions U.S. dollars for the exports in 2022. While EAC is viewed to be lagging behind in the implementation of Customs Union Protocol, SADC has constantly come to the EAC to benchmark and learn from the later. This is because the EAC integration is a progressive single integration not a blended integration like that of SADC and ECOWAS.

Sensitive Items/Products in the EAC

These are products that each country needs in abundance which are scarce in the country. They are then taxed differently and therefore they attract higher tariffs than the 4th tariff bands. These products include milk, which could attract 60% tax; wheat that can attract 35% tax; maize which can be taxed to 50% tax and sugar that can attracts up to 100% taxes given that it is scarce and a basic product for citizens. Much of the sugar from the region is imported from Pakistan.

EAC Single Customs Territory

The EAC Summit of Heads of State and Governments at their Extra-Ordinary meeting on 12th April 2011, agreed in Principle to adopt the *Destination Model* of clearance of goods where assessment and collection of revenue is at the first point of entry and revenues are remitted to the destination partner states subject to fulfillment of key pre- conditions to be developed by the High Level Task Force (HLTF). This High Level Task Force (HLTF) compiled its report, which was approved and adopted by the Summit of Heads of States and Governments in July 2016.

The HLTF was established and identified three pillars for the implementation of the EAC Single Customs Territory as follows:
- Free circulation of goods
- Revenue management systems
- Regional legal and institutional framework

The scope of free circulation of goods considered the following:
- Treatment of goods under free circulation
- Imports into the EAC region
- Goods for direct home consumption
- Warehousing
- Transit
- Temporary Importation

EAC Single Customs Territory Scope of Free Circulations
- Transfer of duty paid goods in a Partner State to another State
- Ex-warehousing between Partner States
- Treatment of goods in Special Economic Zones
- EPZs and Free Ports
- Temporary Transfer
- Transfer of locally produced goods
- Movement of exempted goods and country specific remissions or stay of application of CET among others.

Pre-conditions for Free Circulation
- ICT requirements
- Regional cargo tracking system

- Customs transit guarantee scheme (RCTGS) to enable the operationalization of a regional bond
- Enabling legal and institutional framework for the administration of the Customs IT interface and exchange of information across borders

Revenue Management Systems for Single Customs Territory

The scope of Revenue Management Systems in a Single Customs Territory considered the following:

- Effective payment systems
- Process flows
- Efficiency in clearance of goods
- Confirmation and notification of payments; and
- Reconciliation

Revenue Management Systems Pre-conditions

- ICT requirements
- Cargo tracking system that can be interfaced across the EAC region
- Enabling legal and institutional framework for the administration of the Customs IT interface and exchange of information across borders
- Regional Customs Transit Guarantee Scheme (RCTGS) to enable the operationalization of a regional bond.

Legal and Institutional Framework for EAC Single Customs Territory

The following aspects to be reviewed to cater for the SCT:

- Offences
- Regional bond systems
- Use of ICT systems
- Extra territoriality operations
- Mutual recognition
- Customs legal compliance

Hurdles to EAC Customs Administration

Despite these progress made throughout the years, some challenges remain noteworthy when it comes to the implementation of the EAC Customs Union.

Poor Implementation of CET

This has been challenging to the Partner States. Customs valuation procedures have been varying; resulting in different computed values for taxation. Since 2005, Uganda has produced a list of industrial products that are exempted from the CET. A similar list of industrial inputs is in place for Rwanda and Burundi. Moreover, the United Republic of Tanzania, as a member of both the Southern African Development Community (SADC) and the EAC, has taken integration commitments in both regional contexts, thereby having to implement two CET, one being for EAC and the other for SADC. Likewise, the remaining six members of the EAC are also members of the Common Market for Eastern and Southern Africa (COMESA), thus facing similar challenges as the one encountered by Tanzania in terms of multiple commitments taken in the contexts of various integration agenda.

Selective Implementation of Rules of Origin (RoO)

The implementation has been largely successful in the region, except for a number of challenges where disputes have arisen and verification missions were constituted to address the problems. In the wheat industry, we have for instance observed protectionist tendencies, which have been justified using rules of origin-related arguments. Moreover, efforts in sensitization/awareness-raising seem to have been too limited to allow relevant stakeholders realize the opportunities they could draw from EAC integration.

Slow Internal Tariff Elimination

Although this is an area where the EAC Partner States have scored eighty percent in implementation, it is our anticipation that this achievement will be increase to hundred percent amongst the partner states.

The EAC has undergone great efforts to eliminate Non-Tariff Barriers. Similar efforts have been undertaken at the SADC and COMESA levels, where national and regional structures to monitor and curb NTBs are in place; and have attracted a genuine cooperation between the public and private sectors. There are however a number of NTBs remaining in the EAC as well as in COMESA and SADC: while some have been eliminated, others are mushrooming up. So far 245 NTBS have been eliminated in the EAC region.

The EAC is yet to have a Single Customs Territory (SCT) despite having the protocol in place. Other notable challenges include those emanating from Special Economic Zones (SEZs) and Export Processing Zones (EPZs) regimes as well as those of Investments Promotion Authorities; the delayed adoption of the EAC Industrialization Policy and Strategy, and the long overdue EAC Sanitary Phytosanitary (SPS) Protocol. The realignment or harmonization of EAC laws with that of Partner State continued as a hurdle, which slowed down the full implementation of the customs union. From 2010 to 2022, about 67% of customs union has been implemented by the Partner States. This is due to the principle of variable geometry, which is the progressivity principle of 'build as you live'.

Specific Hurdles of Custom Union Protocol in the Republic of South Sudan

South Sudan is yet to launch and implement the Customs Union Protocol in totality. Although it has trained its custom officers to clear the goods and services on time, the failure to go digital has impeded the implementation of this baby protocol of the EAC. The other challenge is weak institutions, particularly, economic, legal and political institutions to guide on the implementation of the protocol. Above all, the senseless war and insecurity in South Sudan has confounded the implementation of a Customs Union Protocol in realization of a single custom territory that efficiently and effectively cleared goods and services on time.

Other Developments and Challenges: Looking Beyond the Customs Union

The EAC seems to be the most vibrant REC in the southern hemisphere and is tremendously advancing in its integration process: however, crucial issues remain to be addressed.

Sequencing

Despite the challenges encountered in implementing the first stage of integration, that is the EAC Customs Union, the EAC moved on and entered into a Common Market in 2010, after completing the negotiations in 2009. The Common Market Protocol calls for liberalization of the labour market, capital market and services market. The Customs Union Protocol has already liberalized the goods and services market. At time of writing, implementation of the Common Market in EAC has however not gone beyond the 60%. There are several national laws that have to be amended so that they are compatible with the Common Market. Only a few laws have been amended by Partner States so far.

Despite these challenges, the completion of the Common Market negotiations made the EAC proceed forward with the negotiations of the third stage of EAC integration, which is the negotiation of the Monetary Union. Both policy-makers and experts seem to have non-technical reasoning at this stage: the Customs Union has not been fully implemented, the Common Market has gone up to 60%; and yet, the negotiations of the Monetary Union are underway. The negotiators have remained steady on the negotiating timeframes, and have ignored the economic turbulences facing the euro zone's austerity measures and the macroeconomic convergence. As much as EAC can venture in numerous fronts, this one seems to be rather premature.

Economic Partnership Agreements (EPAs)

The EPA Negotiations are taking twists and turns and at some stage, it becoming apparent that the EAC is not sure what it wants in the EPA and how it can achieve it.

EAC – SADC – COMESA Tripartite Grand Free Trade Area

Another development to pay attention to is the potential EAC – SADC – COMESA Tripartite Grand Free Trade Area. Given the situation on the ground in terms of EAC integration and the way the REC is engaging on numerous fronts, it is very likely that it can get to the level of signing the Tripartite Grand Free Trade Agreement and still have basic outstanding issues that need to be solved. The main appeal to the Secretariats of COMESA, EAC and SADC as well as to individual Partner States is to conduct a self-evaluation exercise. It is important to implement the Abuja Declaration and progress in the regional integration agenda. But there is a great need of connecting the regional and national players so that the regional commitments get implemented nationally. The poor state of infrastructure and energy also remain a challenge to a great number of African countries, making intra-African trade very expensive.

Customs administration in EAC has challenges as described above. However, the major setbacks to customs administration and growth are the fact that in the EAC there are summarized as non-tariff barriers, insufficient communication infrastructure and conflicting interests at national and regional levels, including the promotion of trade and investment against revenue maximization. Some initiatives (to mention but a few) the recently established One Stop Border Posts, Single

Window System, ongoing transport infrastructure development, and continual efforts to eliminate non-tariff barriers which ought to ease the functions of Customs and escalate trade facilitation in the region.

Trade Facilitation in EAC Customs Union (CU)

In the EAC CU, as in many other countries, customs plays an important role in international trade. Albeit more other institutions also play their role in international trade. Their activities may have positive and negative impact on trade performance and economic growth depending how they are coordinated. Trade facilitation thus aims at harnessing measures that have positive impacts on trade. Trade facilitation involves different actors to implement a set of rules, guidelines and procedures that promote trade rather than hampering it.

There are a number of definitions of trade facilitation used by different authors and different organizations. The United Nations Economic Commission for Europe (UNECE), for instance, defines trade facilitation as a "comprehensive and integrated approach to reducing the complexity and costs of the trade transaction process, and ensuring that all these activities can take place in an efficient, transparent, and predictable manner, based on internationally accepted norms, standards and best practices." The International Chamber of Commerce considers trade facilitation as relating to improvements in the efficiency of administrative and logistic steps associated with the international trade of goods. Cutting short the list of examples, it is important to stress that many of the various definitions refer to reducing the time and costs of the trade transaction process (Kafeero 2008). A WCO's conventional definition of trade facilitation is "simplification and harmonization of international trade procedures; where trade procedures are the activities, practices, and formalities involved in collecting, presenting, communicating and processing data required for the movement of goods in international trade." Article 75 of the EAC Treaty (1999) establishes the EAC CU calling for trade facilitation.

Indeed, article 75 of the EAC Protocol on establishment of the EAC CU stipulates initiatives for trade facilitation among Partner States; reduction of number and volume of trade documentation, adoption of common standards and documentation, coordination of trade facilitation and transport within the Community, periodic review of procedures, dissemination of trade information, establishment joint training programs on trade, and adoption of common external tariffs. The instruments of trade facilitation in the Community includes: The Treaty, 1999; The Customs Union Protocol, 2005; Customs Management Act, 2005; various legal instruments relating to trade in goods such as Standardization, Quality Assurance, Metrology and Testing (SQMT) Act 2008; Instruments to addressing supply side constraints such as Tripartite Agreement on Road Transport, 2001.

William Khaguli (2013) studied the impact of trade facilitation on eight border posts of the EAC countries, and concluded that the implementation of trade facilitation measures in the EAC has seen the region being able to increase trade flows and boost economic growth (Khaguli, 2013). The OECD (2013) indicates that in some African countries revenue losses from inefficient border procedures are estimated to exceed 5% percent of GDP. These losses are associated largely with trade costs due to complex customs procedures. Automation is reported as one measure of reducing this cost and has a potential to reduce trade costs by as much as 2.9%.

Indicators of Trade Facilitation Performance

The OECD has developed a set of trade facilitation indicators that identify areas for action and enable the potential impact of reforms to be assessed. The OECD indicators cover the full spectrum of border procedures, from advance rulings to transit guarantees, for 133 countries across income levels, geographical regions and development stages. Estimates based on the indicators provide a basis for governments to prioritize trade facilitation actions and mobilize technical assistance and capacity-building

Figure 1: Potential Benefits of Customs Union in Facilitating Trade

Improve border policies and procedures: • Automate • Simplify regulations • Advanced rulings • Appeal procedures	Reduced time delay		Increase share of production for export
			Increase GDP
			Increase trade
Improve transportation: • Infrastructure - road - rail - air - ports • Regulations	Reduced uncertainty	Reduced cost	Increase trade variety
			Increase investment
			Increase tariff collections

Source: Kgrugal, 1999

efforts for developing countries in a more targeted way.

Performance in logistics is important for trade facilitation. Efficient logistics is instrumental to the performance of many of the trade facilitation indicators. The World Bank developed a set of indicators for measuring performance in trade logistics. The Logistics Performance Indicator (LPI) is an interactive benchmarking tool created to help countries identify the challenges and opportunities they face in their performance on trade logistics and what they can do to improve their performance.

ICT Development for Trade Facilitation in EAC Custom Union

In the efforts to simplify goods clearance and reduce trade costs, EAC countries have adopted several ICT systems for simplifying goods clearance. The systems have improved efficiency in clearance procedures by: expediting release time, uniform application of customs law, effective implementation of risk management, efficient revenue collection, effective data analysis and efficient production of trade statistics. These ICT systems have contributed a lot, for instance, by reducing the time for clearance and release. Electronic filing of customs documents has been introduced, document processing has been centralized in Kenya and Tanzania, and the level of transparency has generally increased (Kafeero, 2008). For ease of exchange of information and implementation of the One Stop Border Post (OSBP) initiative adopting a single system by all countries would be ideal.

The establishment of the Single Window System for all stakeholders has remained a challenge for the automation of ICT in customs administration among the EAC Partner States. Kenya is the first country in EAC to establish a Single Window System known as "Kenya TradeNet." Tanzania has introduced Single Window System at the Dar es Salaam Authority while concurrently Customs has adopted a new system called TANCIS (Tanzania Customs Integrated System) which replaces the Automated System for Customs Data (ASYCUDA++). These systems are expected to reduce dwell time at ports and improve the ease of doing business by providing working modules for relevant institutions that do not have adequate Management Information Systems. Rwanda and Uganda have migrated from ASYCUDA++ to ASYCUDA World while Burundi is still using ASYCUDA++. Electronic Cargo Tracking System is also in use in Tanzania to control the movement of high-risk goods by sending either controlled or real time monitoring of goods in transit.

The use of TANCIS in Tanzania is expected to greatly improve the clearance process by providing one platform where all stakeholders involved in the importation and exportation of goods can exchange necessary information. Importers and exporters are expected to submit all the necessary documentation through the platform. Government agencies involved in the goods clearing process (like Tanzania Bureau of Standards, and Tanzania Food and Drugs Authority) can then process those documents and issue the necessary permits and clearances. Clearing agents have access to TANCIS from the comfort of their own offices as long as they have access to the Internet. The system also links in other stakeholders like shipping lines and the Tanzania Ports Authority to speed up the goods clearing processes. Banks have also been linked up to facilitate quick payment of customs fees and duties. As a result of these efforts, the time from lodging of documents to the issuance of Customs release orders at the Port of Dar es Salaam is expected to be reduced from four days to one day. Goods clearance time at the Port of Dar es Salaam was expected to be reduced from five days to one day for exported goods, and from 9 days to 5 days for imported goods.

A study by Tosevska, Trpcevska (2014) on the effects of the implementation of Single Window and simplified customs procedures in the Republic of Macedonia reported that companies evaluate positively the application of the Single Window for obtaining licenses and for tariff quota allocation (Trpcevska, 2014). The greatest benefit realized by the users of the Single Window has been the savings in time and human resources, with a 66.16% reduction. All measured variables - average number of documents, signatures, hours, and financial costs - have been reduced compared to regular customs procedures. Further, the study reported that the reduction in time needed for one simplified customs procedure might have a significant influence on increasing trade and especially exports. Djankov et al (2006) cited in Tosevska-Trpcevska (2014) estimated that a 10% saving in time in preparing to export may result in an increase in exports of 4%, and that each additional day that the goods are held pending clearance decreases trade by at least 1%.

Customs Risk Management for Trade Facilitation
A common characteristic of customs work is the high volume of

transactions and the impossibility of checking all of them. Customs administrators therefore face the challenge of facilitating the movement of legitimate passengers and cargo while applying controls to detect customs fraud and other offences. These competing interests mean that it is necessary to find a balance between facilitation and control.

Customs administrators use risk analysis to determine which persons, goods, and means of transport should be examined and to what extent. Risk analysis and risk assessment are analytical processes that are used to determine which risks are the most serious and should have priority for being treated or having corrective action taken. Risk analysis involves a selection programme that makes use of risk profiles, which have been established in a process of risk analysis and assessment. Risk profiles encompass various indicators, such as; type of goods, traders and their compliance records, value of goods and applicable duties, destination and origin countries, mode of transport and routes which are built based on characteristics displayed by unlawful consignments (or offending passengers).

World Customs Organization (WCO) has developed various tools to assist its member countries in the establishment of profiles and the management of intelligence collection. The WCO Customs Enforcement Network (CEN) database can, for example, provide useful intelligence for the establishment of risk profiles. These profiles then drive inspection selectivity programmes, through which data declared are analyzed on the basis of the identified risk parameters and consignments, and depending on the selected risk level, goods and persons are routed through different channels of Customs control. Consignments and persons considered as 'low-risk' based on the risk profile attract minimal attention and intervention from Customs and can be processed quickly (WCO & UNCTAD, 2008). The TANCIS system for example is capable of identifying and categorizing risk level and uses a color scheme to rank goods to be cleared; green channel for immediate release without examination; yellow channel for those which needs documentary check; red channel for those which require physical examination of goods and documents; and blue channel for examination at a later stage post audit.

The Role of Customs Post-Clearance Audit in Trade Facilitation

According to WCO and UNCTAD (2011), a post-clearance audit means audit-based Customs control performed subsequent to the release of the cargo from Customs' custody. The purpose of such audits is to verify the accuracy and authenticity of declarations and cover the control of traders' commercial data, business systems, records and books. Such an audit can take place at the premises of the trader, and may take into account individual transactions, so-called "trans-action-based" audit, or cover imports and/or exports undertaken over a certain period of time, the so-called "company based" audit. Implementation of post-clearance audit is part of the risk management strategy. Post-clearance audits are often introduced in conjunction with the implementation of automated procedures in Customs oper-ations. However, audit-based control can also be applied in a manual or semi-automated environment.

The WCO (2012) guidelines for post-clearance audit stipulate the objectives of post-clearance audit as: to assure that customs declara-tions have been completed in compliance with customs requirements, via examination of a trader's systems, accounting records and premises; to verify that the amount of revenue legally due has been identified and paid; to facilitate international trade movements of the compli-ant trade sector; to ensure goods liable to specific import/export controls are properly declared, including prohibitions and restrictions, licenses, quota; to ensure conditions relating to specific approvals and authorizations are being observed, for example, pre-authenticated transit documents, the preferential origin/movement certificates, licenses, quota arrangements, Customs and excise warehouses and other simplified procedure arrangements.

Post-clearance audits can be conducted on a case-by-case basis, focusing on targeted operators, selected on the grounds of risk analysis of the commodity and the trader, or in a planned, regular way, set out in an annual audit programme. Furthermore, the audit could also be used as criterion to offer special treatment to certain economic operators. If well-implemented, post-clearance audits are expected to facilitate reduced release time, saving storage and warehouse fees, as well as insurance costs for goods under storage that are automatically reduced. Also it ensures a more efficient control since it can cover all customs regimes – temporary importation, inward processing, duty-free zones, end-use tariff items – and therefore enhance customs control over some of these regimes which could not be checked at the border.

Post-clearance audit can benefit from a broader picture of the transactions over a longer period of time. Details for comparison come from local or national databases and include information from each customs declaration registered. By comparing prices and tariff headings for identical or similar commodities related to different companies, inconsistencies may indicate fraud. Similarly, comparisons between countries of origin or different suppliers or pattern of intra-company trading may reveal false declarations. If the audit detects an incorrect declaration, the audit officer can ask for the correction of the declaration. This may entail an additional payment of duties or taxes by the trader and even raise customs' revenues.

Customs audit has proved effective in facilitating trade and counteracting customs offenses in many countries and thereby improving customs and tax compliance. In Korea for example, a customs team detected violations such as tax evasions or false declarations, bringing in about 100 million USD in additional revenues in 2019, and approximately 480 million USD in 2020, which in return motivated importers to more carefully and accurately declare their goods (WTO,

2021). Despite these potential benefits, a post clearance audit has a number of challenges in developing countries. One of these challenges is availability of skilled labour. A report by Rajkarnikar (2007) on the implementation of WTO Customs Valuation Agreement in Nepal, indicated that lack of trained manpower for audit purpose has significant impact on realizing result of post-clearance audit. The study concluded that audit manual is necessary to implement the post clearance audit.

Transport Infrastructure and Trade Cost in EAC Customs Union

Efficient transport infrastructure is another important factor for trade facilitation and performance of businesses. Shorter and more predictable transport times can cut costs, raise profits, and allow product diversification. Upgrading transportation infrastructure, including ports, railways, roads, and air transport, is crucial for increasing trade. As a result, dealers in a given product who cannot be sure when the next shipment will arrive, they must often spend more to keep extra supplies of the product in stock. This problem erodes the profits of businesses all over Sub-Saharan Africa. Variability in transport times also discourages African businesses from exporting goods that are sensitive to delays, such as fresh horticultural products (USITC, 2012).

The EAC Regional Transport Strategy, (2011) indicates that the surface transport modes provide the main transport links with neighboring countries and within the EAC. Most of the EAC countries are landlocked and depends on the two major ports of Dar es Salaam (Tanzania) and Mombasa (Kenya). Unfortunately, the countries located at the coast are large thus coordinating infrastructure in one country is already a huge task and doing it across borders is even more difficult. Andrea Balisteri et al. (2014) categorized trade costs into three areas; costs that can be lowered by trade facilitation, non-tariff barriers, and the costs of business services (Balisteri, 2014). Andrea Balisteri (2014) emphasized "there is substantial evidence that with the progressive global decline in tariffs over several decades, trade costs are a more significant barrier to trade than tariffs, especially in Sub-Saharan Africa" (Ibid). A report by IMF in 2014 on "Regional Economic Outlook for Sub-Saharan Africa" shows that most Sub-Saharan African countries have made limited transport infrastructure development; as a result transport cost are very high. Transport and insurance costs represent an average of 30% of the value of exports whereas in landlocked countries like Rwanda, these costs may reach up to 50% of total exports value. No wonder then, that high transport costs, caused by infrastructure deficiencies, delays, fees or procedures are encountered in the transit country, make the land leg of the shipping of goods to landlocked countries very costly and oblige the landlocked country to maintain high levels of inventory. For most landlocked countries, high transport costs remain the single most important obstacle to their equitable access to global markets and competition with other countries.

Challenges of Trade Facilitation

Trade facilitation has the potential to promote competitiveness and market integration. Moreover, trade facilitation can make multilateral trade liberalization an important tool for development in a system based on predictable rules, openness and lack of discrimination (Cosgrove-Sacks & Apostolov 2003). Despite the potential and successes of trade facilitation there are also challenges of implementing trade facilitation in Africa. The obstacles to trade facilitation are not only many and varied, but they are also inter-related. This situation requires an integrated, cooperative response from the Government and the private sector. Andrea Buyonge and Barnaba Kireeva (2008) highlighted some of these challenges which include the lack of a service attitude across all customs management levels, adversarial relationship between customs officers and businessmen and women, insufficient or inefficient supporting infrastructure, lack of a facilitation culture in other government departments, corruption and illicit trade. A holistic approach is thus needed to address trade facilitation as some of the impediments are crosscutting and cannot be addressed by a customs department alone.

Performance in Trade Facilitation

Most EAC countries are faring well in trade facilitation when compared with Sub-Saharan Africa and low-income countries across a number of indicators. However, performance is far lower when bench-marked with a best practice country such as Singapore (USAITC, 2012). Tanzania is performing best compared to other EAC countries in terms of internal border agency cooperation and automation while Kenya is performing better than the rest of EAC countries on external border agency cooperation. Tanzania is not doing well compared with other EAC countries in terms of governance and impartiality. Governance issues such as corruption negatively affect trade facilitation and are associated with increased cost of doing business and reduced competitiveness. Rwanda and Uganda are doing best in information availability. Information availability increases transparency and thus counteracts poor governance issues such as corruption. Information availability also increases consistence of application of procedures, reduce transaction costs and improve fairness. Further, results indicate that Tanzania is performing well its involvement in the trade community as compared to the rest of EAC countries. This has impacted on instilling ownership and cooperation between the government and other stakeholders and hence smoothens implementation of various policies that are aimed at improving trade and customs administration. Andrea Buyonge and Barnaba Kireeva (2008) observed that most customs administrators find it difficult to sustain genuine dialogue with business, and the relationship is mutually antagonistic because compliance with customs laws and procedures is often involuntary.

The World Bank (2021) report on ease of doing business ranked

South Sudan 186, Burundi 165, Uganda 101, Tanzania at 76, Kenya at 58 and Rwanda 11 out of 189 global economies on performance in trading across borders. This ranking compares countries in terms of efficiency in export and import procedures by comparing documents, time and cost for exportation and importation. These ranks imply that EAC countries are not performing well compared to the rest of the world, calling for measures for further improvement in trade facilitation. However, Rwanda has remained outstanding, in being the best country in Africa to do business in.

Challenges of Customs Union in Trade Facilitation

Non-Tariff Barriers (NTBs) are the major setback to trade facilitation. A report by EAC (2021) on the status of elimination of non-tariff barriers in EAC indicates that the elimination of NTBs is incomplete. While there are new NTBs and old unresolved, 245 NBTs have been eliminated so far. Other challenges of trade facilitation include level of transport infrastructure, which resulted in poor infrastructure that delays goods in transit, and increased transport costs. Reliance on roads and low investment in railway has further increased trade costs due to low economies of scale on road transport. The One-Stop Border Post concept has been developed and being applied by Partner States. However, customs and non-customs procedures are not harmonized and there is lack of legal mandate of the EAC secretariat to enforce trade facilitation instruments. Likewise, there is low capacity both in terms of human and financial resources for effective implementation of trade facilitation. The financial support from donors for trade facilitation is very small. It is the EU that has constantly helped with meager funds to build capacities for trade facilitation in the EAC.

Most EAC countries have multiple memberships outside EAC, for example in COMESA, SADC and ECCAS. Tanzania for instance has membership in EAC, COMESA and SADC. On the other hand, DR Congo has membership in EAC, COMESA, SADC and ECCAS.

The objectives of these blocks are sometimes conflicting. There is inconsistency in the sensitive products lists – excluding products from liberalization. Also we have non-compliance to Rules of Origin as a result of challenges of documentation and non-recognition of certificates of origin from other Partner States.

Integrity of implementing agencies has continued to pose significant challenges. Customs division in EAC countries is implicated with a number of integrity issues such as corruption and fairness in assessment of duty for imported goods. As Customs is an important fiscal area in EAC, there is a challenge of balancing between trade facilitation and control. Capacity for Customs audit is very low which necessitate auditing of very few companies as a result unfaithful companies takes advantage of this low capacity.

Members of Sectoral Council on Customs and Labour during the consultative discussions at Hilton Hotel, Nairobi on 15th July 2017

Reflections on Common Market Protocol (Social Integration and Mobility of Labour) in the EAC: The Journey and the Next Steps

A Common Market (Soko La Pamoja in Swahili) is an arrangement where member countries of a REC, for example, EAC operate as a single market for goods, services, labour and capital, and having common tax and common trade laws. A common market integrates the factors of production (labour, goods, services, capital, right of establishment), which were not integrated by individual member states into one single market. The protocol contains 56 articles and 6 annexes.

Common Market Protocol Provides for Five Freedoms and Two Rights:

- The free movement of goods;
- The free movement of persons
- The free movement of labour
- The free movement of service; and
- The free movement of capital.
- The right of establishment

However, this book analyses free movement of workers, labour and right of establishment as below.

The Free Movement of Workers

The EAC Treaty, article 104 and the EAC Common Market Protocol (CMP), articles 5, 7, 8 and 9, 13 & 14 has empowered the EAC Partner States citizens to enjoy the free movement principles as persons within a Common Market. Free movement cuts across almost all the freedoms and rights making migration one of the most important fundamental pillars of the Common Market. Articles 5, 7, 8, 9, 10,11,12, 13 & 14 of the EAC Common Market Protocol oblige Partner States to implement the following principles in enhancing free movement of persons in a migration context:

- Ease cross border movement of persons and eventually adopt an integrated border management system – Article 5(b);
- Article 5(c), remove restrictions on the movement of labour, harmonize labour policies, programs legislations, social services, provide for social security benefits for workers, and establish common standards and measures for the association of workers and employers, establish employment promotion centres and eventually adopt a common employment policy;
- Article 5 (d), remove immigration restrictions to the right of establishment & residence of nationals of other Partner States in their territory in accordance with the provisions of this Protocol;
- Under Article 7 (1) – the Partner States hereby guarantee the free movement of persons who are citizens of the other Partner States, within their territories;
- Article 7 (2) goes further to state that Partner States shall ensure non discrimination of the citizens of the other Partner States based on their nationalities by ensuring that:

    I.   The entry of the citizens of the other Partner States into the territory of the Partner State without a visa;

    II. Free movement of persons who are citizens of the other Partner State within the territory of the Partner State;

    III. That the citizens of the other Partner State are allowed to stay in the territory of the Partner State as they wish; and

    IV. That the citizens of the other Partner States are allowed to exit the territory of the Partner State without restrictions.

Under Article 8 of the EAC, CMP, Partner States undertook to establish a common standard system of issuing national identification documents to their nationals, which shall be the basis for identifying the citizens of the Partner States within the Community.

In accordance with Article 9, a citizen of a Partner State who wishes to travel to another Partner State shall use a valid common standard travel document, and Partner States, which have agreed to use machine-readable and electronic national identity cards as travel documents may do so. The Partner States, which have agreed to use machine-readable and electronic national identity cards, have been granted the freedom to work out the modalities for implementation. For instance, all the seven Partner States of the EAC have been directed by the Summit of the Heads of States to allow citizens to use their national identifications documents (IDs) to cross over and move freely amongst the seven Partner States.

Articles 10, 11, 12, & 14 provisions lay the foundation for the movement of workers - both formal and self-employed and the attendant rights of establishment and residence.

How Have the Provisions of Free Movement of Persons Facilitated Social Integration in the Community?

At the regional level, the EAC Council of Ministers (CoMs) has taken various decisions and directives to facilitate the free movement of people. These includes:

- The introduction of the old machine readable EA passport in 1999 which was upgraded by Partner States in 2017 to the new East African e-passport after the launch by the Summit of the Heads of States.
- Establishment of a sub committee comprising of Partner States' Chiefs of Immigration and Chiefs of National Intelligence Services as the technical arms on regional Immigration matters;
- Conducting joint training and development of human resource capacities with the Partner States Departments of Immigration
- Having a common regime of travel documents
- Reciprocal opening of border stations

- Use of Common Entry/Exit declaration Forms
- Operationalization of 12 One Stop Border Posts (OSBPs) to facilitate faster movement of both Persons and Goods
- Removal of fees for student passes for nationals of other Partner States studying in the region.
- Establishment of exclusive traveller clearing booths at all E/E Points for East Africans.
- Payment of uniform hotel accommodation rates/Game Park Entry fees for EAC Partner states citizens;
- Harmonisation of higher education fees for students studying in educational institutions in all Partner States & Establishment of the Inter-University Council for East Africa for purposes of higher education curricula harmonization & Quality Assurance.

Other measures, which have facilitated the social integration agenda, include – the use of machine-readable and electronic IDs as travel documents. Under article 9, Partner States have the option to use national ID cards as travel documents provided that they work out the modalities. Nevertheless, the use of the ID is still a challenge in the region as not all Partner States have shown real initiative to actualize the commitment between 2010 and 2022. Only the Republics of Kenya, Rwanda & Uganda have agreed to do so at the time of writing this book.

The number of citizens issued with standardized machine-readable National ID's out of the eligible population varies from one Partner State to another. In Rwanda, the count of citizens who have been issued with machine -readable IDs is around 7.2 million out of a population of 12.5 million citizens. The Republic of Uganda has issued national IDs to over 17.2 million Ugandans aged 16 years and above and 9 million Ugandan children below the age of 16 years have also been registered for issuance of National Identity cards out of the total recorded population of 40 million Ugandans (2018 Census).

The United Republic of Tanzania established a National Identification Authority in 2013, with the objective of registration and issuance of IDs to their nationals. The exercise of issuance of IDs is still an on-going process. For the Republic of Burundi, the country signed a contract with a vendor to design and produce 6 million National Biometric Identity Cards, within 5 years, to produce standardized electronic machine-readable national IDs. Republic of South Sudan produces its machine-readable national identification cards for her citizens. It is the Democratic Republic of Congo who is yet to produce machine-readable IDS for its citizens.

The Republic of Kenya undertook a massive registration process and about 95% of the eligible population was covered, and the process of upgrading her ID card system started towards the end of 2018. The Republic of South Sudan has established the institutional framework under the Nationality Act, 2011 and decree No 09/2011 to register and issue IDs (national certificates) and e-Passports (The EAC, CMP 2018)

Nevertheless, the use of the ID is still a challenge in the region as not all Partner States have shown real initiative to actualize the commitment between 2010 and 2020. Only the Republics of Kenya, Rwanda & Uganda have agreed to do so.

Pursuant to the directive of the 17th Ordinary Summit of the EAC Heads of States for Partner States to commence issuance of the New EA e-Passport, by 31st January 2018, Partner States commenced the issuance of the EA e-Passport during the period September 2017 to 1st July 2019. The Republic of Kenya commenced the issuance of the EA e- Passport on 1st September 2017; the United Republic of Tanzania commenced the issuance of the EA e-Passport on 31st January 2018; Republic of Burundi commenced the issuance of the EA e-Passport on 31st May 2018; The Republic of Uganda commenced the issuance of the EA e- Passport on 18th December 2018; and the Republic of Rwanda commenced the issuance of the EA e-Passport on 1st

July 2019. The Republic of South Sudan is still putting in place the necessary infrastructure and systems to commence the issuance of the EA e-Passport.

The new EA e-Passport facilitates movement of East African within the region and internationally.

Entry/Stay and Exit of Citizens

In accordance with regulation 5 (1) of Annex I of the EAC Common Market (Free Movement of Persons) regulations, a citizen of a Partner State who seeks to enter or exit the territory of another Partner State shall do so at the entry or exit points designated in accordance with the national laws of the Partner States and comply with immigration procedures. A citizen of one Partner State can enter another Partner State as long as he or she can prove his or her citizenship using a National Identification Card. Regulation 5 (3) of Annex I of the EAC Common Market (Free Movement of Persons) regulations, entitles citizens of a Partner State to enter into a territory of the host Partner State and stay up to Six Months. The Partner States have demonstrated a remarkable commitment through the amendment / establishment of laws or administrative procedures that entry/exit of Partner States citizens into the territories of each other as shown in Table 3 below.

Table 3: Trend of Number of Citizens Moving from Other Partner States Granted Stay

Period	Burundi	Kenya	Rwanda	RSS	Tanzania	Uganda
2013	191,972	309,982	371,273		575,317	1,153,936
2014	177,112	147,427	334,482		329,335	1,157,881
2015	93,087	354,136	528,955		205,502	878,292
2016	103,699	194,459	3,350		708,998	419,611
2017	76,114	403,507	572,355		413,526	1,380
2018	73,084	501,428	816,822		371,140	2,164
2019	72,611	500,994	596,118	56,594	499,331	410,515
2020	29,535	203,405	209,771	62,742	212,174	412,959

Source: EAC Secretariat CMP Implementation Data, 2020

Stay of Students

Regulation 6 (1), stipulates that a citizen who is admitted as a student in an approved training establishment of another Partner State shall apply for a student pass. The data collected from 2010 to 2018 shows that, a number of students granted *gratis* student passes to stay in a host Partner State show steady increase by each of the Partner States. This is linked to the easing of the visa requirement and Partner States efforts to harmonize educational system in the region as a result of systematic implementation of the commitments under the CMP.

Table 4: Trend of Number of Students Granted Gratis Student Passes

Period	Burundi	Kenya	Rwanda	South Sudan	Tanzania	Uganda
Jan–June 2011	Kenya: 0 Rwanda: 0 RSS: 0 Tanzania: 0 Uganda: 0	Burundi: 90 Rwanda: 159 RSS: 0 Tanzania: 445 Uganda: 348	Burundi: 866 Kenya: 4 RSS: 0 Tanzania: 3 Uganda: 10	0 N/A 0 N/A 0 N/A 0 N/A 0 N/A	Burundi: 0 Kenya: 51 Rwanda: 13 RSS: 0 Uganda: 25	Burundi: 57 Kenya: 720 Rwanda: 291 RSS: 0 Tanzania: 559
Jan–June 2015	Kenya 22 Rwanda 615 RSS: 0 Tanzania 15 Uganda 9	Burundi: 67 Rwanda: 83 RSS: 0 Tanzania: 209 Uganda: 134	Burundi: 678 Kenya: 26 RSS: 0 Tanzania: 51 Uganda: 50	0 N/A 0 N/A 0 N/A 0 N/A 0 N/A	Burundi: 12 Kenya: 113 Rwanda: 103 RSS: 0 Uganda: 83	Burundi: 87 Kenya: 424 Rwanda: 208 RSS: 0 Tanzania: 282
Jan–June 2018	Kenya: 11 Rwanda: 72 S. Sudan: 0 Tanzania: 7 Uganda: 2	Burundi: 61 Rwanda: 81 RSS: 0 Tanzania: 281 Uganda: 236	Burundi: 1601 Kenya: 36 RSS: 0 Tanzania: 33 Uganda: 55	Burundi: 0 Kenya: 0 Rwanda: 0 Tanzania 0 Uganda: 0	Burundi 7 Kenya 68 Rwanda 9 RSS: 0 Uganda 50	Burundi 101 Kenya 201 Rwanda 136 RSS: 0 Tanzania 245

Source: Adapted from Framework of M&E – Implementation of CMP, 2018

Harmonization of National Immigration Policies and Laws

Article 47 of the Common Market Protocol mandates Partner States to approximate their national laws and harmonise their policies and systems for purposes of implementing the Protocol. The positive aspect is that the Partner States have demonstrated their commitment to amending the restrictive laws as agreed and directed by the Council. A review of the list of discriminatory laws that have been amended/enacted by a Partner State to guarantee the Free Movement of Persons since July 2010 to date shows varying levels of actions by the Partner States.

In 2010, Burundi initiated amendments on its Immigration policy. Further action was taken to develop a draft law on the Immigration law in 2014, followed by undertaking Administrative procedures amended through Ordinance (N°215/1855 of the 20th November 2012) in 2015. Further amendments were effected on Administrative procedures on: Residence permit; months stay to be decentralized; *Décret-Loi N°1/007 du 20 Mars 1989 portant réglementation de l'accès, du séjour et de l'établissement des étrangers sur le territoire du Burundi et de leur éloignement.*

In responding to the commitments, in 2019 Kenya initiated amendment of the Immigration Act (Cap 172); Alien Restriction Act (cap 173); Registration of Persons Act (Cap 107) and Foreign Nationals Management Service Act 2011. By 2013 amendments were effected by Uganda on Citizenship and Immigration control The Immigration Act, 1995; and Act, CAP 66. South Sudan has issued Immigration Regulations from Immigration Act 2011. Immigration Act 2011 is yet to be amended.

Other Initiatives Supporting the EAC Social Integration Agenda

The Implementation of the Consultative Dialogue Framework for Private Sector and Civil Society participation in the EAC integration process, 2012 and the Annual EAC Secretary General's Forum is an initiative, which is complimenting the implementation of the EAC CMP and Treaty provisions under Article 127. The continuous and people-centred dialogue of the private sector, civil society, local governments, and other interest groups has facilitated the involvement and participation of non-state actors and the general citizenry in the EAC integration process:

The Conferences on the Role of Women in Socio-Economic Development and in Business has resulted into awareness creation and empowerment of women. So far, these have resulted in the creation of the East African Women in Business Platform (hosted by the East African Business Council).

Establishment of the East African Youth Network (EAYN) as a regional network of youth civil society organisations and together with Political Affairs department, the establishment of an EAC Youth Ambassadors Platform (EAYP) made of selected youth ambassadors with a mandate of sensitizing students from Higher Institutions of Learning about the EAC integration process has so far yielded fruits in terms of social integration.

The Implementation of the bi-annual EAC culture and arts festivals commonly known as JAMAFEST & the EAC sports editions, the inter-parliamentary games held by EALA, The military games; the annual students essay writing competition have also contributed greatly to the movement of persons and the social integration agenda of the people of East Africa.

Therefore social integration is a highly desirable outcome that reflects the existence of social cohesion, a strong institutional foundation and a culture of acceptance. East Africa is better off today as the

Community implements the various stages of integration and with its mantra–*one people, one destiny.*

Challenges Encountered in Regard to the Free Movement of Workers

From the analysis of the provided tables, Partner States have made great strides in the facilitation of the free movement of persons. However, challenges abound, as the granted freedoms are not always granted. These challenges include:

a. Delayed harmonisation and approximation of Partner States' nationals immigration laws and related policies;

b. The rights provided under Articles 10 and 13 to workers and self-employed persons have been granted under national laws.

c. The use of IDs as travel documents have not been embraced by all Partner States.

d. Lack of continuous capacity building for immigration officers of the Partner States on the agreed upon regional legal frameworks that facilitate the free movement principles and therefore some restrictions on movement of persons are witnessed on various occasions.

e. The development of Council directives & regulations to govern enjoyment of the rights. The decision making process in the Community takes a long time.

Free Movement of Workers

Under Article 10 of the Common Market Protocol, Partner States guaranteed free movement of workers, who are citizens of the other Partner States, within their territories. The free movement of workers shall entitle a worker to: apply for employment and accept offers of employment actually made; move freely within the territories of the Partner States for the purpose of employment; conclude contracts and take up employment in accordance with the contracts, national laws and administrative actions, without any discrimination; stay in the territory of a Partner State for the purpose of employment in accordance with the national laws and administrative procedures governing the employment of workers of that Partner State; enjoy the freedom of association and collective bargaining for better working conditions in accordance with the national laws of the host Partner State; enjoy the rights and benefits of social security as accorded to the workers of the host Partner State; and have the right to be accompanied by a spouse and a child (family unification)

Free movement of labour comprises of a worker and a self-employed person. A worker is a holder of a contract while a self-employed person is one that seeks to undertake an economic activity in another Partner State other than that of his or her origin (CMP Interpretation Part A). Both the worker and the self-employed person have the right to move, to take up and pursue economic activities in the territory of the other Partner State and as a self-employed person, to establish his or her company, firm in the territory of the other Partner State. The worker or self-employed person can also reside in the other Partner State in accordance with the provisions in the CMP and its accompanying regulations. The freedom of movement as a worker or as a self-employed person is guaranteed in the EAC through a series of basic principles, following international practice on these types of commitments:

Employment and Remuneration Without Discrimination Based on their Nationalities

To facilitate employment and remuneration without discrimination, Partner States since July 2010 have worked progressively to remove laws that are restrictive and discriminatory to the movement of labour from one Partner State to another. In 2010, Uganda had the most of laws (11 in total) for restricting citizens of other Partner States in relation to employment, remuneration and other conditions of work and employment. Kenya had five laws, while Burundi had three laws. By 2018 the situation had improved with only Uganda retaining one such law. The Framework of M&E – Implementation of CMP, 2018 has demonstrated that a number of laws restricting citizens of other Partner States in relation to employment and remuneration have been eliminated. This is good for regional integration.

Application and Issuance of Work Permits

Under the EAC Common Market Protocol, Annex II, Regulation 6, Partner States committed to implementing procedures in their national legislations that (1) enable EAC citizens to access work permits, (2) allow the issuance of a special pass for workers with contracts not exceeding 90 days, (3) allow issuance of special pass for workers with contracts of more than 90 days, as they await a work permit, (4) allow issuance of permits for workers with a contract of more than 90 days, within 30 days of application and valid for two years and renewable upon application, (5) allow use of the harmonized classification of work permit and forms, fees, and procedures, and (6) require annual employer returns to be submitted to the competent authority of the Partner State.

The number of work permit applications received from citizens of other Partner States increased systematically during the last eight years of the Common Market Protocol (CMP) implementation. The highest number of work permit applications was received by Rwanda, followed by Kenya (*Refer to Table 5 below*). This active work permit received from different Partner States is an important precursor for regional integration and cross–border economic engagements and improved business-friendly environment in the region.

Temporary work permits for high-skilled individuals exceed 30 days in all EAC Partner States except Rwanda. For countries with an undersupply of engineers, computer professionals, doctors, and the like, this presents a productivity problem. Allowing access to each other's workers can help alleviate such pressure, at least in part.

Table 5: Work Permits Issued to EAC Citizens in Partner States

Period	Burundi	Kenya	Rwanda	Tanzania	Uganda
2013	35	1,097	4,740	1,274	847
2014	24	1078	2,547	960	624
2015	16	939	2,254	–	817
2016	34	913	2,996	549	739
2017	25	1,045	3,609	1,192	895
2018	24	2,873	2,645	568	769
2019	0	1,367	0	1,123	623

Source: Adapted from Framework of M&E – Implementation of CMP, 2018

An analysis of the number of work permit applications from citizens of other Partner States shows that the rejected or deferred permit applications were minimal. It is worth noting, however, that the fees for residence and work permits have been harmonized for EAC Partner States except in Tanzania & Burundi. Uganda had removed the fees or reduced them to zero but has reneged on its position and is now charging. The trend is generally encouraging. Tanzania has reduced the processing and issuance of work permit to three working days. South Sudan doesn't have data for the work permits issued to the EAC Partner States.

Workers' Rights to be Accompanied
by a Spouse, Children and Dependants

Article 10 (5) and (6) of the EAC Common Market Protocol provides for the entitlement of a worker, to be accompanied by a spouse, children and dependants. However, in 2010 no data on spouses, children and dependants accompanying the workers was available. This started to change in 2015 when a number of spouses, children and dependants started to accompany the workers (*Refer to table 6 below*). This is an indication of the possible impact from the implementation of the commitments in this area by the Partner States. In 2018, the higher number of spouses, children and dependants accompanying a worker/self-employed person from other Partner States increased markedly.

Table 6 indicates that the number of spouses accompanying workers/self-employed persons from other Partner States is generally low. This can be explained by the nature of the self-employment business that requires more time to stabilize in order to settle the accompanying family members. It is necessary to consider, within the framework of CMP, the long-term possibilities to stabilize the operations for the self-employed as they settle in the environment of the receiving Partner States.

Table 6: Number of Spouses, Children and Dependants Accompanying a Worker

Period	Burundi	Kenya	Rwanda	South Sudan	Tanzania	Uganda
Jan–June 2010	Kenya: 0	Burundi: 0	Burundi: 0	N/A 0	Burundi: 5	Burundi: No Data 0
	Rwanda: 0	Rwanda: 0	Kenya: 0	N/A 0	Kenya: 85	Kenya: 0
	RSS: 0	RSS: 0	RSS: 0	N/A 0	Rwanda: 2	Rwanda: No Data 0
	Tanzania: 0	Tanzania: 0	Tanzania: 0	N/A 0	RSS: 0	RSS: N/A 0
	Uganda: 0	Uganda: 0	Uganda: 0	N/A 0	Uganda: 11	Tanzania: 0
Jan–June 2015	Kenya: 0	Burundi: 0	Burundi: 0	N/A 0	Burundi: 0	Burundi: 11
	Rwanda: 0	Rwanda: 0	Kenya: 0	N/A 0	Kenya: 0	Kenya: 111
	RSS: 0	RSS: 0	RSS: 0	N/A 0	Rwanda: 0	Rwanda: 14
	Tanzania: 0	Tanzania: 0	Tanzania: 0	N/A 0	RSS: 0	RSS: N/A 0
	Uganda: 0	Uganda: 0	Uganda: 0	N/A 0	Uganda: 0	Tanzania: 13
Jan–June 2017	Kenya: 0	Burundi: 12	Burundi: 86	Burundi: 0	Burundi: 0	Burundi 17
	Rwanda: 0	Rwanda: 13	Kenya: 161	Kenya: 0	Kenya: 0	Kenya 133
	RSS: 0	S. Sudan: 5	RSS: 0	Rwanda: 0	Rwanda: 0	29
	Tanzania: 0	Tanzania: 25	Tanzania: 18	Tanzania: 0	RSS: 0	RSS 0
	Uganda: 0	Uganda: 24	Uganda: 66	Uganda: 0	Uganda: 0	Tanzania 13

Source: Adapted from Framework of M&E – Implementation of CMP, 2018

Table 7: Number of Spouses Accompanying Workers/Self-Employed Persons from Other Partner States

Period	Burundi	Kenya	Rwanda	South Sudan	Tanzania	Uganda
Jan–June 2010	Kenya: 0	Burundi: 0	Burundi: 0	Burundi: N/A	Burundi: 0	Burundi: 0
	Rwanda: 0	Rwanda: 0	Kenya: 0	Kenya: N/A	Kenya: 0	Kenya: 0
	RSS: 0	RSS: 0	RSS: 0	Rwanda: N/A	Rwanda: 0	Rwanda: 0
	Uganda: 0	Uganda: 0	Uganda: 0	Uganda: N/A	RSS: 0	RSS: 0
	Tanzania: 0	Tanzania: 0	Tanzania: 0	Tanzania: N/A	Uganda: 0	Tanzania: 0
Jan–June 2015	Kenya: 0	Burundi: 0	Burundi: 55	Burundi: N/A	Burundi: 0	Burundi: 4
	Rwanda: 0	Rwanda: 0	Kenya: 87	Kenya: N/A	Kenya: 0	Kenya: 52
	RSS: 0	RSS: 0	RSS: 0	Rwanda: N/A	Rwanda: 0	Rwanda: 6
	Uganda: 0	Uganda: 0	Uganda: 80	Uganda: N/A	RSS: 0	RSS: 0
	Tanzania: 0	Tanzania: 0	Tanzania: 18	Tanzania: N/A	Uganda: 0	Tanzania: 5
Jan–June 2018	Kenya: 0	Burundi: 0	Burundi: 0	Burundi: 0	Burundi: 0	Burundi: 6
	Rwanda: 0	Rwanda: 0	Kenya: 0	Kenya: 0	Kenya: 0	Kenya: 40
	RSS: 0	RSS: 0	RSS: 0	Rwanda: 0	Rwanda: 0	Rwanda: 10
	Uganda: 0	Uganda: 0	Uganda: 0	Uganda: 0	RSS: 0	RSS: 0
	Tanzania: 0	Tanzania: 0	Tanzania: 0	Tanzania: 0	Uganda: 0	Tanzania: 14

Source: Adapted from Framework of M&E – Implementation of CMP, 2018

Coordination and Harmonization of Social Security Policies, Laws and Systems

The provisions of Article 10 3(f); 10 (4) and 12 (3) of the EAC Common Market Protocol relates to the enjoyment of workers & self employed workers the right to social security and mandates the Council of Ministers to issue directives and make regulations on coordination of social security benefits for the workers. A draft Council directive, which was developed during the negotiation period of the Common Market Protocol, was presented to the 22nd Meeting of Council of Ministers held on 15th April 2011 for consideration. The Council noted that there were challenges facing the development of a directive on the coordination of social security benefits in the EAC at that time due to the following challenges: different social security schemes, different periods of coverage, different contribution rates and number of social security branches of benefits covered by a scheme and lack of legal provisions to port accrued social security benefits across schemes both at national and the regional levels.

Where as during that period Partner States implemented the CMP, the National Social Security Funds have initiated the necessary legal reforms/enactment of new laws to address some of the identified challenges, extend coverage of social protection at national level and the process of developing the EAC Council directive on the Coordination of Social Security Benefits have begun. The new draft EAC Council directive which aims at coordinating portability of four Social Security benefits at regional level – will include the: old-age or retirement benefit; disability/invalidity benefit; survivors' benefit & health insurance.

Coordination means a mechanism(s) that will allow the implementation of five fundamental principles identified in International Labour Organisation Conventions and Recommendations and in particular,

- *Equality of treatment* (eliminating restrictions, based on nationality, on a person's social security rights and obligations under the legislation of any of the Partner States);
- *Export of benefits* (ensuring the payment of benefits to persons in a Partner State other than the Partner State under whose legislation a right to a benefit has been established);
- *Determining the legislation applicable* (ensuring workers and self employed persons moving within the East African Community will be subjected to the legislation of only one Partner State by eliminating situations in which a person would otherwise have to contribute to the social security systems of two Partner States for the same worker);
- *Aggregation of periods,* often referred to as totalizing (adding together periods of coverage or insurance in two or more Partner States to fulfil the contributory requirement for a benefit under the legislation of any Partner State);
- *Mutual assistance* among the social security authorities and institutions of the Partner States to give effect to the four principles specified above.

Mutual Recognition of Academic and Professional Qualifications

Under Article 11 of the EAC Common Market Protocol, the EAC Partner States undertook to mutually recognize the academic and professional qualifications granted, experience obtained, requirements met, licenses or certificates granted in the other EAC Partner States.

Annex VII, to the EAC Common Market Protocol on mutual recognition of academic and professional qualifications regulations, has been concluded and is undergoing legal review and input by the Sectoral Council for Legal and Judicial Affairs

Although the EAC Partner States undertook to mutually recognize academic and professional qualifications, as an enabler to the free movement of workers, this area has remained the most restricted commitment for the free movement of workers, where all Partner States scored 0 in the 2018 score card on the free movement of workers. Nevertheless, there are some positive developments on mutual recognition agreements (MRAs) that have been signed and are actually under implementation. This includes the MRA for Architects, Accountants, Engineers, Veterinarians and Lawyers.

The number of workers from other Partner States whose academic qualifications, experiences obtained, licenses and certifications had been recognized by each Partner State. Recognition was improved in 2015 when a number of Partner States started to acknowledge academic qualifications, experiences obtained, licenses and certifications from the other Partner States. By the second half of 2018, an upsurge of the recognition of academic qualifications, experiences obtained, licenses and certifications was noticeable in all Partner States.

Right of Establishment

The Partner States under Article 13 of the CMP guarantee the right of establishment of nationals of the other Partner States within their territories and to ensure non-discrimination of the nationals of the other Partner States, based on their nationalities. This entitles nationals in the region to take up and pursue economic activities as self-employed persons and set up and manage economic undertakings in the territory of another Partner State.

The CMP further under Article 11(1a) provides that the Partner States shall mutually recognize the relevant academic and professional qualifications granted, experience obtained, requirements met, licenses and certificates granted to a company or firm in the other Partner States. Partner States are expected to ensure that workers who are citizens of a Partner State employed in the territory of another Partner

Table 8: *Workers from Other Partner States whose Academic Qualifications, Experiences Obtained, Licenses and Certifications Have Been Recognized by 2010*

Period	Burundi	Kenya	Rwanda	South Sudan	Tanzania	Uganda
Jan–June 2010	Kenya: 0	Burundi: 0	Burundi: 40	N/A	Burundi: 0	Burundi: 0
	Rwanda: 0	Rwanda: 0	Kenya: 126	N/A	Kenya: 0	Kenya: 0
	RSS 0	RSS: 0	RSS: N/A 0	N/A	RSS 0	RSS: 0
	Tanzania: 0	Tanzania: 0	Tanzania: 25	N/A	Rwanda: 0	Rwanda: 0
	Uganda: 0	Uganda: 0	Uganda: 272	N/A	Uganda: 0	Tanzania: 0
Jan–June 2015	Kenya: 0	Burundi: 12	Burundi: 19	N/A	Burundi: 0	Burundi: 2
	Rwanda: 0	Rwanda: 29	Kenya: 10	N/A	Kenya: 0	Kenya: 212
	RSS: 0	RSS: 0	RSS: 0	N/A	RSS: 0	RSS: 0
	Tanzania: 0	Tanzania: 199	Tanzania: 0	N/A	Rwanda: 0	Rwanda: 6
	Uganda: 1	Uganda: 217	Uganda: 49	N/A	Uganda: 0	Tanzania: 273
Jan–June 2018	Kenya: 3	Burundi: 43	Burundi: 21	Burundi: 0	Burundi: 0	Burundi: 3
	Rwanda; 2	Rwanda: 85	Kenya: 28	Kenya: 0	Kenya: 0	Kenya: 283
	RSS 0	Sudan: 10	RSS: 0	Rwanda: 0	Rwanda: 0	RSS: 29
	Tanzania: 0	Tanzania: 152	Tanzania: 5	Tanzania: 0	S. Sudan: 0	Rwanda: 9
	Uganda 0	Uganda: 230	Uganda: 38	Uganda: 0	Uganda 269	Tanzania: 10

Source: Adapted from Framework of M&E – Implementation of CMP, 2018

State are allowed to remain in that territory for the purpose of taking up economic activities as self-employed persons.

The implementation of this article is in accordance with the annexes to be concluded by Partner States, a process that have not been concluded by Council. The draft annex on mutual recognition of academic & professional qualifications is still undergoing legal review & input under the Legal and Judicial Sectoral Council.

Identifying policies, laws and regulations that hinder the guarantee of the right of establishment

Partner States have agreed that policies, laws, regulations and any requirements that amount to hindering the right of establishment are to be identified and abolished. This commitment is mandatory as it influences the implementation of other commitments related to right of establishment. In general, the information on economic undertakings in a Partner State that have been set–up and owned by citizens of the other Partner State has been rather slow. This commitment calls for actions by each of the Partner States to establish mechanisms to handle complaints on restrictions on companies and firms from other Partner States in relation to the right of establishment. A lot more work, however, needs to be done by the Partner States to facilitate the implementation of this commitment.

Right of Residence

The CMP requires a Partner State to guarantee the right of residence to the citizens of the other Partner States who have been admitted in their territories in accordance with Articles 10 and 13 and this right applies to the spouse, child and a dependent of a worker or self-employed person. The Partner States are expected to issue residence permits to citizens of other Partner States who qualify in accordance with the provisions of this article. The implementation of this article shall be in accordance with the East African Community Common Market (right of residence) Regulations, specified in Annex IV to the CMP. The Partner States agreed that access to and the national policies and laws of the Partner States shall govern the use of land and premises, which is pertinent to the right of establishment and right of residence.

There have been positive developments in the region in regard to rights of residence. Table 8 below indicates that the number of residence/ work permits that were issued by a Partner State to workers and self-employed persons who qualify in accordance with article 14 has steadily increased over the trend period. This is a positive signal for regional integration. The number of work permit applications received from citizens of other Partner States increased systematically from 2010 to 2019. The highest number of work permit applications was received by the Republic of Rwanda and followed by Kenya (refer to the table 9 below). This work permit applications received from different Partner States is an important precursor for regional integration and cross-border economic engagements and improved business - friendly environment in the region.

Various researches have also documented that temporary work permits for high-skilled individuals exceed the stipulated 30 days issuance period in all EAC Partner States except in the Republic of Rwanda.

The assessment of EAC Partner States' performance in the implementation of the commitments made on the free movement of workers commitments is discussed comprehensively in the scorecard for 2018. On average, EAC Partner States scored 56% in the implementation of the crosscutting commitments on the right of establishment and residence. The lead Partner States in the implementation of these commitments was Rwanda, Kenya and Burundi, with scores of 71%, 57% and 57%, respectively. Tanzania follows with 52%, and Uganda with 45%. South Sudan and DR Congo don't have data yet.

Table 9: Residence/Work permits issued
to EAC Citizens in Partner States

Period	Burundi	Kenya	Rwanda	Tanzania	Uganda
2013	35	1,097	4,740	1,274	847
2014	24	1078	2,547	960	624
2015	16	939	2,254	–	817
2016	34	913	2,996	549	739
2017	25	1,045	3,609	1,192	895
2018	24	2,873	2,645	568	769
2019	0	1,367	0	1,123	623

Source: EAC Common Market Monitoring Framework 2018

Table 10. Performance on Workers Commitments by Partner States

CMP Commitment	Number of Indicators	Scores Per Cent (%)					
		BUR	KEN	RWA	UGA	TZ	Regional Average
Free movement of workers (CMP Article 10 (1) to (9))	5	60	40	80	80	60	64
Workers freedom of entry, stay and exit (Annex II, Regulation 5(1) to (6))	2	100	0	100	100	100	80
Procedures for acquiring work permit (Regulation 6)	6	50	83	83	17	60	59
Procedures related to denial of a work permit (Regulations 7 (1-4))	3	67	100	67	100	100	87

CMP Commitment	Number of Indicators	Scores					
		Per Cent (%)					
		BUR	KEN	RWA	UGA	TZ	Regional Average
Procedures related to cancellation of work permit (Regulation 8 (1-2)	2	50	50	100	100	50	70
Access to employment opportunities (Regulation 12 (1) 7 (2)	2	100	50	50	0	0	40
Equal treatment in employment (Regulation 13)	1	100	100	100	100	100	100
h) Monitoring of labour market (Regulation 14 (1))	1	0	100	100	0	0	40
Harmonization and mutual recognition of academic and professional qualifications (CMP Article 11 (1) ((a)-(b))	2	0	0	0	0	0	0
Right of residence (Article 14)	1	100	100	100	0	100	80
Harmonization of labour policies, laws and programs (CMP Article 12(1)	1	0	0	0	0	0	0
Total	26	57	57	71	45	52	56

Source: East Africa Common Market Scorecard 2020

Table 10 provides an overall scoring of EAC Partner States against an overall EAC regional average. The assessment of EAC Partner States' performance in the implementation of these commitments is discussed in the Scorecard for 2018. On average, EAC Partner States scored 56% in the implementation of the crosscutting commitments on the right of establishment and residence. The lead Partner States in the implementation of these commitments was Rwanda, Kenya and Burundi, with scores of 71%, 57% and 57%, respectively. Tanzania follows with 52%, and Uganda with 45%. Republic of South Sudan is not captured there because the country by then did not formally implement the protocol.

The main reason behind the low performance level relates to the slow development of the regional framework for harmonization of labour policies, laws, and programs. The Scorecard further illustrated that the fundamentals behind non-implementation of the commitments on 'removal of restrictions' and 'certifications' as key causal factors behind this low performance.

Challenges in the Implementation of the Common Market Protocol

The challenges identified by the various studies undertaken to assess the implementation of the EAC Common Market Protocol and especially in regard to the free movement of persons and workers can be categorized into 4 categories: Legal, Administrative, Social and Financial.

Legal Challenges

They are discussed as follows:
a. Delayed harmonisation and approximation of Partner States' nationals labour laws and related policies;
b. The rights provided under Article 10 and 13 to workers and self-employed persons have not been granted under national laws.
c. While the development of Council directives & regulations govern enjoyment of the rights, the decision making process in the Community takes long time;
d. Harmonisation of the classification of work permit/residence fees, forms and procedures remain a conundrum;
e. Putting in place a framework to enable mutual recognition of professional and academic qualifications;

f. Delayed finalization of the mechanism to allow the exchange of young workers; and

g. Delayed finalization of the Draft EAC Council Directive on the coordination and portability of social security benefits

Administrative Challenges

a. Mutual recognition of professional qualifications, licensing of establishments and issuance of work permits. The process is also pegged under national laws;

b. Enforcement of concluded mutual recognition agreements is - left to national chapters of the professional associations/bodies; and

c. Lack of reliable facts and figures to facilitate planning to inform decision making:

Social Challenges

a. Lack of awareness by the citizens of the Partner States on the EAC integration agenda; the benefits & opportunities offered by the CMP; the provisions of the CM and citizens obligations in support of the regional integration agenda.

b. The unequal past development of human resources which make some Partner States fear the movement of workers.

Financial Challenges

a. Inadequate allocation of resources (human & financial) to the implementation of the EAC Common Market Protocol at national and regional levels.

b. Financing of the Community projects & programmes over the years has become more donors driven than through Partner States budget allocation.

Proposed Interventions

- Partner States should be directed to prioritize the harmonization of labour policies, laws and programmes and Immigration policies and laws that are not yet aligned to the EAC CMP;
- Conclusion of the delayed process of finalizing & implementing a harmonized classification of work/residence permit fees and procedures for approval by the Council in accordance with Annex II, Regulation 6 (9) of the Protocol;
- Council to expedite the adoption by Council of Annex VII - Mutual Recognition of Academic and Professional Qualifications to provide the necessary legal framework to conclude Mutual Recognition Agreements;
- Partner States to conclude the process on the harmonization of education curricula examinations, standards, certification and accreditation of educational and training institutions;
- Partner States should promote and enhance the existing social dialogue needed to support labour mobility and coordination of social security benefits between the social partners - Governments, workers and employer associations in the region;
- EAC in collaboration with the ministries responsible for EAC Affairs in the Partner States to undertake regular awareness creation sessions on the benefits of the EAC Common Market; the opportunities offered by the Protocol and citizens obligations in the implementation of the Protocol;
- Partner States to allocate the required resources at both national and regional levels to support the implementation of the CMP and to support the work of the national implementation committees;
- EAC Partner State expedites the conclusion of on-going discussions on the coordination of social security benefits. As a first step, Partner States should review their national social security & social health insurance policies and laws to facilitate the conclusion on

the draft EAC Council directive on the coordination and portability of social security benefits;

- Partner States to agree to implementation the developed framework for a joint programme on the exchange of young workers
pursuant to Article 10 (8) of the Protocol; and

- To realise the benefits of an EAC Common Market, Partner States
may consider adopting a regional law on the implementation of
the EAC Common Market Protocol - a good practice that has
greatly helped to realise the benefits of the EAC Customs Union
at a faster rate.

Next Steps into the Future

The free movement principles of the EAC CM Protocol will continue
to dictate the EAC integration agenda.

The EAC regional integration process is also providing interesting
lessons for other Regional Economic Communities at continental
level.

The challenges cited earlier should be seen as opportunities for
all East Africans to exercise the freedoms & rights enshrined in the
protocol and for Governments to create an enabling environment for
the achievement of a functional CMP.

The formation of national Committees on the Implementation of
the Common Market Protocol have provided much needed guidance
in terms of monitoring implementation of the Common Market
Protocol provisions and educating the public on the same;

However, involvement/sensitization of parliamentarians (regional
& national), private sector and civil societies is key in disseminating
information on the benefits of the regional integration agenda.

South Sudan Plan of the Implementation of Common Market Protocol (CMP)

Table 11: Draft Schedule for the Free Movement of Workers to South Sudan (Not Yet Implemented)

Category of workers				Implementation Dates
Major groups	**Sub- group**	**Minor groups**	**Occupational titles**	
Professionals	Physical, Mathematical and Engineering Science Professionals	Physicists, Chemists and Related Professionals, Mathematicians, Statisticians and Related Professionals, Computing Professionals Architects, Engineers and Related Professionals	PhD	2016/17
	Life Science and Health Professionals	Life Science Professionals	Biologist, Botanist, Zoologist, Ecologist, Veterinary Professionals	2016/17

Category of workers				Imple-mentation Dates
Major groups	Sub- group	Minor groups	Occu-pational titles	
		Health Professionals	Medical Doctor, Medical Research Officer, Dentist	2016/17
		Nursing and Midwifery Professionals	Specialised Nurses	2016/17
	Teaching Professionals	University Teachers	PhD, Masters level, where appropriate, Researchers	2016/17
	Other Teaching Professionals	Technical and Vocational Higher Education Teachers Technical Institute Teachers and Instructors	PhD, Masters level, Researchers	2016/17

Category of workers				Imple-mentation Dates
Major groups	**Sub- group**	**Minor groups**	**Occu-pational titles**	
	Other Professionals	Business Professionals, Archivists, Librarians and Related Information Professionals, Social Science and Related Professionals, Writers and Creative or Performing Artists,		2016/17
		Religious Professionals	Minister of Religion	2016/17
Technicians And Associated Professionals				

Category of workers				Imple-mentation Dates
Major groups	**Sub- group**	**Minor groups**	**Occu-pational titles**	
Adminis-trators and managers	Directors and Chief Execu-tives	Directors and Chief Execu-tives	Managing Directors Chairman, Company,	
			Direc-tor-Gener-al, Corpo-ration	
			Director, Managing / Compa-ny Direc-tor	
			Compa-ny Chief Executive	

Source: Ministry of East African Affairs-RSS

The Status of Implementation of Monetary Union Protocol (Common Currency)

The Monetary Union Protocol (MUP) was signed on the 30th November 2013 in Kampala-Uganda. The Heads of States and Governments agreed to implement this protocol in November 2023. This gives a grace period of 10 years for the preparation and setting up of the relevant institutions for the implementation of the Monetary Union Protocol. The East African shilling was agreed as the common currency for the region. The institutions for trainings are already established. This includes the East African Institute of Banking in Uganda and other fiscal and monetary - related schools in the region including the Institute of Monetary Studies, which is being turned into the University of Monetary Studies in Ruaraka-Thika Road in Nairobi-Kenya. Institutions of regional banking such as the East African Development Bank and the East African Central Bank have already been established. The importance of the MUP/Common Currency Protocol is to enhance convergence criteria for the difference currencies in the region. This is for easy and timely trade amongst the Partner States.

However, the Challenge to the MUP is that Partner States in the region use different currencies such as the shilling for Kenya, Tanzania and Uganda and france for Rwanda and Burundi and pound for South Sudan. This is going to make convergence criteria quite difficult. Apart from different currencies, the economic developments amongst the seven Partner States are quite different with countries such as Burundi and South Sudan leading the Partner States in levels of poverty. Whereas the Heads of States scheduled the implementation of the MUP to November 2023, however, the indication that it will be implemented in 2023 has not been forthcoming. Early dissemination of the MUP by Partner States should be done given that 2023 at the time of writing is less than a year away.

The Author during the High Level Summit on the 11 Years of
Implementation of Common Market Protocol
held in Arusha on 20th July 2022.

The Author during the High Level Summit on the 11 Years of
Implementation of Common Market Protocol
held in Arusha on 20th July 2022.

The Political Federation/Confederation Protocol

The Political Federation is the ultimate goal of the EAC regional integration, the fourth step after the Customs Union, Common Market and Monetary Union. It is provided for under Article 5(2) of the Treaty for the Establishment of the East African Community and founded on three pillars: common foreign and security policies, good governance and effective implementation of the prior stages of regional integration.

The Concept of Federation

A federation can loosely be defined as a form of Government or country where there is territorial distribution of power between one central or a common government and subordinate or lower Governments. The elements of a federation therefore, include shared powers and responsibilities defined by law and practice. It therefore goes without saying that in order to federate, federating units should be prepared to cede certain powers to one common center. This perhaps is the most important of all prerequisites for a successful federation to take place.

The visionary purpose for the establishment of an East African Federation is the accelerated economic development for all, to enable the region to move away from a least developed region to a developed region, in the shortest possible time. The purpose of an East African Federation is best described by the following quotations:

"The balkanization of Africa into 54, mostly sub-optimal States, has meant that Africa cannot have a large internal market under one Political Authority; have no power to negotiate with the rest of the world. This balkanization must stop"- H.E. Yoweri Kaguta Museveni, President, Republic of Uganda

"We have everything to gain in East African Federation in terms of political stability, greater feeling in safety in numbers and as an economic entity

better able to fight poverty" - H.E. Benjamin William Mkapa President, United Republic of Tanzania

"I firmly believe that regional integration is not a choice but a necessary strategy for sustainable development. On a cultural level, regional integration solidifies the unity of communities with personalities and common history, language and culture" - H.E. Mwai Kibaki President, Republic of Kenya

There is a general appreciation for a United East Africa with a stronger economy that would guarantee people jobs, better standards of living and pride of belonging to such an ideal State. In the age of information technology, people are increasingly exposed to the conditions of life in the developed parts of the world, which at best they can only imitate. The people express, therefore, a brave and bold vision of a federation that would be competitive in the era of globalization. In order to realize high and sustainable growth trends in the federation, there should be commitment to timely, effective and time-bound decisions together with their implementation.

Arguments for Political Federation

When societies merge to form one large economic and political entity, issues of tribalism, religious and other socio-cultural problems would tend to disappear slowly; this has proven difficult under each separate country.

The federation will remove any possibilities of Partner States fighting each other and as more countries later join the federation, the political stability of the region will further be entrenched given that the tribal and ethnic groups' feelings will be tightly controlled, discouraged and unity of the ethnic groups promoted by the federal government.

A political federation is imperative in this global environment. But for federation to survive there must be an environment that enables people to participate in an accelerated economic development process, and economic development can be made faster within a political federation than when it is done under totally separate state governments just like the case of the great United States of America.

Expectations from EAC Political Federation

General Political Expectations

The expectations with regard to the political aspects of EAC federation relate to pride in belonging to a vast and powerful region that would command respect and a stronger voice in the world; and that would support security, peaceful co-existence and prosperity. The federation is expected to get rid of all manner of ethnic and sectional conflicts. The people expect the federation to address, more effectively the issues of security, governance, etc in the EAC, and establish lasting solutions.

General Economic Expectations

The expectations with regard to the economy relate to acceleration of economic growth with the resultant benefits of uplifting the standards of living for all. Furthermore, there would be efficient management of resources and economies of scale, which should generate wealth and create employment. The federation would stimulate development and sharing in the field of education, science and technology which is at the cutting, edge of socioeconomic transformation.

Lake Victoria would be managed as a single and indivisible resource, equitably shared among the East African people. The Lake would be rationally managed, particularly with regard to the imperative to protect and conserve its environment.

General Social Expectations

The people of East Africa look forward to improved social interaction, peaceful coexistence and harmony among neighbors, particularly border communities, with tribalized and ethnic conflicts receding into the past. In particular, they anticipate better governance, democratic and accountable institutions. Education and health services are among the important areas where the federation is expected to make a positive impact.

Federation would pave the way for the rule of law and a strong sense of constitutionalism to take root amongst the Partner States. The sovereignty of the people over the federation should be entrenched through, among others, the institution of referendum to establish the East African Federation.

Expectations of Ordinary Citizens

Ordinary citizens expectations is as follows:

a.   Free movement, right to employment, residence and ownership of property;

b.   Non-discrimination in service provision and fee payments (e.g. school fees, medical and hotel accommodation etc);

c.   Re-unification of communities and families living along the borders;

d.   Peace and security for the pastoralist communities along borders by way of reduced crime, amelioration of economic hardships, and assurance on food security;

e.   The Lake Victoria communities expect beneficial and sustainable utilization of the Lake Victoria resources;

f.   Improved governance through wider democratization, freedom of speech and association;

g.   Standardized education systems;

h.   Participation in the Federal process through a referendum and subsequent direct elections.

i.   Food security;

j.   Single currency; and

k.   Use of a common language, Kiswahili in all Partner States.

Expectations of the Governments and the Bureaucrats

a. It will be a great opportunity to address social and economic imbalances thus generating economic benefits;

b. Stabilization in security matters (terrorism, crime and drugs and arms illicit traffickers);

c. Exploitation of synergies and removal of duplications; and

d. Macroeconomic convergences and harmonization of policies, standards, laws and regulations.

Expectations of the Politicians

a. Political and social stability, in particular elimination of tribalism;

b. Alliances between political parties across borders;

c. Federation forming the nucleus in the integral process towards the realization of the African Union;

d. Common foreign policy; and

e. Retention of some political power at the State level.

Expectations of the Business Community

a. Bigger markets for trade and investment;

b. Increased competition and competitiveness;

c. Reduction in business costs;

d. Increased business opportunities;

e. Free movement of goods and services;

f. Total Elimination of NTBs;

g. Price Stability; and

h. Ease of access to services at Mombasa and Dar es Salaam for landlocked Partner States.

Expectations of Civil Society and Professional Societies

The Civil Society and Professional Associations expect to play robust roles in:

a. Advocacy and sensitization of the citizenry towards the Federation; and

b. Ensure entrenchment of human rights, environmental conservation and setting up of conflict resolution mechanisms.

Fears, Concerns and Challenges (FCCs) in the Adoption of Political Federation

Political and Legal FCCs

a. Sovereignty and Nationalism. The fear is manifested in a number of ways including; notions of loss of political power, loss of decision making, and loss of flexibility in exercising powers at the national level:

b. Collapse of the earlier EAC. This is still fresh in the minds of some people and there is no adequate assurance yet that the past experience will not reoccur;

c. The disparities in the national constitutions and practices of democracy, good governance, anti-corruption, human rights, constitutionalism and the rule of law;

d. People need assurance that they will be involved in the process of making major decisions that touch on their livelihood, including electoral processes;

e. Lack of uniformity in doctrine, discipline and accountability among agencies dealing with peace, security and defense in the Partner States;

f. Concern that the political federation agenda is driven by the political leadership to satisfy political motives;

g. Fear of increase in cross border crime including small arms and light weapons (SALW), illicit drugs, human trafficking;

h. The fear of authoritarian leaders in the region taking up political federation and use it to advance their selfish interests; and

i. The serious concern is on over emphasis on political federation may obscure other stages of integration, as provided for in the Treaty, which are the foundation for a firm political federation.

Economic Fears, Concerns and Challenges (FCCs)

a. Financial sustainability of the proposed political federation with the implied increase in taxation to run one additional tier of government;

b. Weak economies will be dominated by the stronger economies in the region in the absence of a mechanism to address imbalances and ensure equitable distribution of benefits;

c. There is a concern that the differences in the levels of economic development, entrepreneurial skills and competitiveness in the manufacturing and service industries will disadvantage some Partner States;

d. The need for a mechanism to address purchasing power parity as we move towards the monetary union;

e. Domination in the labour market by more skilled and qualified labour force to the disadvantage of nationals;

f. The need to establish mechanisms for sustainable utilization and conservation of the environment;

g. The need for mechanisms for sustainable exploitation of natural resources and equitable distribution of benefits thereof;

h. People are concerned about the differences in the land tenure systems obtaining in the Partner States and how they will be addressed;

i. The need for mechanisms for addressing liabilities contracted by the partner States before the federation i.e. debts, which the EAC Treaty stipulates that it should not be more than 25% of a country GDP.

j. The customs union is faced with a number of operational problems that need to be addressed; and

k. The need to harmonize economic policy reforms.

Social-Cultural FCCs

a. In the absence of national identification documents for some Partner States' citizens, it will be difficult to establish the common identity of East Africans;

b. The fear of losing the gains already made in affirmative action for marginalized groups in the bigger entity;

c. There is a concern that fewer women than men are involved in the decision making of the integration process and this can be confounded in a political federation; and

d. Differences in education systems, curricula and academic/professional qualifications and social welfare schemes among the Partner States.

Solutions to Overcome the FCCs

a. Continuous sensitization programmes about the EAC integration process.

b. Embark on the process of drafting an East African Constitution to clearly define the model of the federation and the distribution of power at various levels.

c. Accelerating and fast tracking of the Customs Union, Common Market, Monetary Union and finally the Political Federation.

d. Promotion of close cooperation in culture and sports and development of indigenous languages.

e. Elaboration of the East African civic education and sensitizations programme to promote the East African identity and solidarity.

f. Promotion of the alternative/home-grown dispute resolutions and peace building mechanisms.

g. Restructure and transform the EAC Secretariat to be able to enforce implementation of decisions of policy organs.

h. Develop a mechanism for equitable distribution of economic benefits to the grassroots.

i. Consolidate and strengthen the relevant polices aimed at building a strong, credible and sustainable federation.

Next Steps into the Future

Political integration is a qualitatively deeper form of integration than economic integration. Achieving its requires the pillars of political federation, that is, a common foreign policy, peace and security, and good governance to be established and strengthened. It also requires structural transformation of regional policies, institutional arrangements and capacities to support the deeper goal of development.

However, the legitimacy and sustainability of the East African Political federation will depend on the extent to which development is achieved. What is critical for a successful federation is a positive environment characterized by among other factors, a strong political will, commitment and the existence of viable regional structures.

It is worth noting that the attainment of a political federation is a process and not an event. Though the process has been slow, the EAC Heads of States resolved at a Special Summit held in Nairobi on 27-29th August 2004 to examine ways and means of deepening and accelerating the process through a fast-track mechanism. The Summit set up a Committee to fast track the EAC Political Federation, Dubbed the *Wako Committee*, its purpose was to carry out wide consultations and finalise the work on the Political Federation. The Committee presented its report to the Summit on 29th November 2004.

As a result of the consultative process, the office of Deputy Secretary General responsible for Political Federation was established in 2006 to coordinate this process.

Since 2004, the EAC has been putting in place initiatives to fast-track political integration. Summit directives were given and national consultations with stakeholders were held between 2006 and 2008. Various studies were also undertaken to examine, facilitate and fast track the process. In the consultations, it became clear that East African citizens wanted to be adequately engaged and to have a say in the decisions and policies pursued by the East African Community.

On 20th May 2017, the EAC Heads of States adopted the Political Confederation as a transitional model of the East African Political Federation.

CHAPTER SIX

South Sudan Accession and
the Quest for EAC Integration

South Sudan's EAC Accession: Key Events:

- November 2011: President Salva Kiir signed an Application for South Sudan's Membership in the EAC.
- April 2012: EAC *Verification Mission* arrived at Juba, South Sudan to establish RSS level of conformity with criteria for Admission of foreign countries. The mission concluded that Republic of South Sudan met some criteria for Admission (*Excerpts from Aggrey Tisa Sabuni, the then Minister of Finance-RSS*).
- August 2013: EAC's Council of Ministers passed a resolution to start work of formal process of negotiations for South Sudan's Accession to the Community. The resolution tasked Ministers of EAC affairs to constitute a High-Level Negotiation Team (HLNT). Its mandate was to negotiate South Sudan Accession to EAC Treaty.
- EAC Partner States were to nominate three members of HLNT by 30th September 2013
- November 2013: South Sudan sent a High-Level mission to EAC

Secretariat at Arusha Tanzania. Going forward, South Sudan was requested to establish relevant counterpart structure to negotiate EAC Accession.

- Mid-November 2013: EAC's High-Level Negotiations Team met the Government of South Sudan then accepted to create relevant negotiations structures for the Accession process.

- March 2014: President Salva Kiir issued the Republican Decree No. 12/2014 forming a High-Level Committee to Negotiate the Republic of South Sudan's Accession to the EAC. The formal process of EAC Accession then began.

- June 2014: The EAC Secretary General with members of the Secretariat then visited South Sudan and engaged with South Sudan stakeholders.

- October 2014: President Salva Kiir via a Republican Decree appointed a Secretary General for South Sudan's Accession to EAC and a docket now changed to Undersecretary of the Ministry of East African Community Affairs.

- March-November 2015: South Sudan Negotiation Secretariat, Technical Committee and High-Level Committee negotiated the Accession of the nascent state to the Community.

- 15th April 2016: President Salva Kiir Mayardit assented to the Treaty of EAC. South Sudan was admitted as the sixth member of the Community amidst fanfare and ululations. The flag of the Republic of South Sudan commenced flying at the EAC head-quarters in Arusha.

- 6th October 2016: South Sudan ratified the instrument of accession and deposited them with the EAC Secretariat and the relevant continental and regional organizations.

South Sudan Process of Accession to the EAC

The processes of Accession were quite breath taking. At the verification levels by the EAC Secretariat, the country was subjected to these few questions, which were answered by the South Sudan technical teams and compiled in two volumes. **In volume one, the following questions were asked:**

1. The Treaty on the Establishment of the East African Community provides for the principle of people-centred and market-driven integration. What measures are in place to ensure adherence to that principle in the integration process?

2. Is the Republic of South Sudan ready to take part in joint financing of EAC Activities, programmes and projects?

3. How is the Republic of South Sudan prepared to join the EAC Customs Unions and Common Market?

4. How is the Republic of South Sudan addressing the problem of over-dependence on oil i.e. how to diversify the resource base?

5. What mechanisms/structures/programmes exist for private sector participation in economic development? What are the legal and institutional frameworks that the Republic of South Sudan has in place to support the private sector development?

6. Which regional and international organizations involved in trade and customs matters/cooperation is the Republic of South Sudan a member to?

7. What is the status on the development of a trade policy and what does the Republic of South Sudan envisage to be the main pillars of the Policy?

8. What are the main imports and their sources? What are the main exports and their destinations?

9. What customs tariff structure is applicable in the Republic of South Sudan and what would be the impact if the Republic of South Sudan adopted the EAC traffic regime?

President Salva Kiir and late President John Pombe Magufuli of Tanzania, former Chair of EAC during the admission of South Sudan into the EAC on 6ᵗʰ October 2016 in Dar es Salaam

10. What is the customs administration/institution structure for the Republic of South Sudan?

11. What laws and regulations are in palace to support market liberalization?

12. Does the Republic of South Sudan have an Industrialisation Policy and Strategy?

13. What measures are in place to create conducive investment climate?

14. What is the progress made by the Republic of South Sudan in developing quality standards for goods?

15. What is the level of development of the institutional capacity in the Republic of South Sudan to oversee the implementation of quality standard?

16. Is the Republic of South Sudan ready to participate in joint promotion of investment for the Region?

17. Does the Republic of South Sudan have an Investment law and relevant Institution?

18. What are the main instruments that the Republic of South Sudan is using to implement its monetary policy?

19. What measures have been put in place to control inflation in the economy?

20. Is the Republic of South Sudan agreeable to the macro-economic convergence criteria as a pre-requisite to implementation of the monetary union and which measures are being put to achieve this?

21. What is the current system/structure of domestic taxes in the Republic of South Sudan?

22. Is the Republic of South Sudan willing to align its budget process to the one of EAC?

23. Is the Republic of South Sudan willing to adopt the EAC Agreement on Avoidance of Double Taxation and Fiscal Evasion (DTA)?

24. What are the tax treaties that the Republic of South Sudan has already concluded with other countries?

25. What measures have been put in place to strengthen the National Bureau of Statistics?

26. Is the Republic of South Sudan willing to harmonize concepts, definitions and dissemination in order to produce regional timely and comparable data?

27. What measure has the Republic of South Sudan put in place to liberalise and develop the finance sector?

28. Will the Republic of South Sudan accept and agree to implement the already signed Protocols and Agreements in the various infrastructure sub-sectors?

29. Does the Republic of South Sudan have projects, plans or strategies for infrastructure development linking it to the EAC or in cooperation with EAC Partners states?

30. Is the Republic of South Sudan willing to co-share the budgets

of the common institutions under infrastructure as provided for their establishing protocols?

31. Is the Republic of South Sudan willing to co-share the budgets of the common institutions under infrastructure as provided for their establishing protocols?

32. Is the Republic of South Sudan willing to adopt, where practicable, standards already developed in the EAC Infrastructure Sub-sectors?

33. Is the Republic of South Sudan a Member or has applied for the Memberships in the following key institutions, COMESA, WTO?

34. Does the Republic of South Sudan have Aviation Primary Law, and is willing to adopt the Harmonised EAC regulations and Technical Guidance Materials and Liberalisation of Air Services?

35. Has the Republic of South Sudan developed regulations and requirements for Aircraft Accident Investigation Procedures?

In volume two, the following questions were asked:

1. How is the Republic of South Sudan prepared to accept the Community as set out in the Treaty?

2. If the Republic of South Sudan is not admitted as a full member, is it ready to join the Community as an associate or as an observer?

3. Is the Republic of South Sudan committed to the principle of equitable distribution of benefits and costs of integration? In which way is the Republic of South Sudan prepared to contribute to the integration process and what benefits do they envisage?

4. The Treaty on the Establishment of the East African Community provides for the Principle of people-centred and market-driven integration. What measures are in place to ensure adherence to that principle in the integration process?

5. What measures will the Republic of South Sudan put in place to ensure the achievement of the Objectives of the Community?

6. Is the Republic of South Sudan ready to designate a ministry in

charge of EAC Affairs upon admission and when?

7. Is the Republic of South Sudan ready to confer upon the legislations, regulations and directives of the Community and its Institutions?

8. Is the Republic of South Sudan ready to accept that the community organs, institution and laws shall take precedence over similar national ones on matters pertaining to the implementation of the Treaty?

9. Is the Republic of South Sudan ready to take part in joint financing of EAC Activities, programmes and projects?

10. What is the time frame when the Republic of South Sudan hopes to conclude the constitution-making process?

11. How does the Interim Constitution cater for universally accepted principle of good governance, democracy, rule of law and observance of human rights?

12. What measures has the Republic of South Sudan put in place to promote national unity, reconciliation and healing?

13. What measures are in place to demobilize, disarm and reintegrate the ex-combatants and militias?

14. Has the Republic of South Sudan put in the place policy and institutional framework for the promotion of security and stability?

15. What is the role of state governments on matters relating to regional integration such as Good Governance, Trade, and Security?

16. What is the progress on the establishment of the key governance institutions such as a permanent Electoral Commission and an Anti-corruption body?

17. What mechanisms/programmes/proposals does the Republic of South Sudan have to address: Security concerns of East Africans living and working in the Republic of South Sudan? Issues of instability including the proliferation of elicit small arms and light weapons?

18. What are the measures in place to enhance the promotion of the Rule of Law?

19. How does the Republic of South Sudan plan to provide for a functioning independent judiciary that can ensure a comprehensive justice system?

20. What measures are in place to strengthen the governance institutions?

21. Does the Republic of South Sudan have national policies, strategies and legislation in the areas of agriculture, food security, natural resource management, and energy?

22. Does the Republic of South Sudan have energy infrastructure plans and strategies to link with EAC?

23. Is the Republic of South Sudan willing to align national policies and strategies to the EAC Agriculture, Environment and Natural Resource Management tourism and energy instruments?

24. Will the Republic of South Sudan accept and agree to ratify and implement the already signed Protocols?

25. EAC has adopted a Common classification of Hotels and other accommodation facilities with a common training curriculum for assessors. Will the Republic of South Sudan be willing to accept these?

26. EAC hosts a Petroleum Conference and Exhibition every two years on a rotational basis. Is the Republic of South Sudan willing to take part and facilitate its officers to a regional steering committee to organize the Conference? Is the Republic of South Sudan willing to host the Conference? Each Ministry of Energy contributes 40,000 USD towards the conference over the above the normal subscriptions to the EAC budget. Is the Republic of South Sudan willing to make this contribution? Each Partner State organises a field trip during the conference. Is the Republic of South Sudan willing to bear the costs associated with organizing the field trip?

27. The EAC is in the process of establishing a centre for Renewable Energy and Efficiency. Is the Republic of South Sudan willing to be part of it?

28. The EAC is in the process of establishing an EAC power pool to coordinate the planning and operation of power system in the region. Is the Republic of South Sudan willing to be part in this arrangement?

29. The EAC has a Cross-Border Electrification Programme where border communities can be supplied with electricity from a neighbouring EAC partner state. Is the Republic of South Sudan willing to be part of the arrangement?

30. The EAC has a power Master Plan, Refineries Development Strategy, Cross-Border Policy and Model Power Supply Agreement, Regional Strategy on Scaling-Up Access to Modern Energy Services. Will the Republic of South Sudan adopt these?

31. When does the Republic of South Sudan plan to establish key Institutions such as a National Environmental Management Authority?

32. What is the status of the Republic South Sudan's application to be part other regional and international Multilateral Agreements (MEAs) including involvement in keys continental policy making platforms such as AMCEN, AMCOW, NEPAD?

33. What are the measures/mechanisms the Republic South Sudan has put in place to manage trans-boundary ecosystems?

34. Is the Republic of South Sudan Energy Sector open for joint investment?

35. Is the Republic of South Sudan party to the Convention on Elimination of all Discrimination against Women (CEDOW) and the Beijing Action Platform?

36. If yes, how far has the country gone with initiating and implementing programmes on women's empowerment e.g. on attainment of the required 30% minimum benchmark of political positions?

37. What initiative does the Republic of South Sudan have in place on the diaspora in national development programmes?

38. What mechanisms does the Republic of South Sudan have in reintegrating refugees and returnees?

39. What are the programmes in place to address the paucity of human resources?

40. What are the programmes in place for enhancing awareness about the EAC?

41. Does the Republic of South Sudan have a National Higher Education Regulatory System with an autonomous institution for that purpose? If there is none, how is higher education regulated? When will an independent regulatory agency be established? Is there a national qualifications framework that harmonizes qualifications in the Republic of South Sudan?

42. How is higher education in the Republic of South Sudan structured in terms of student admission and exit requirements?

43. How is higher education in the Republic of South Sudan financed? What is the fees structure and levels?

44. Is the Republic of South Sudan's ready to adopt the already agreed policies on harmonization of fees for East Africans and mutual recognition of academic and professional qualifications?

45. What measure is in place to promote science and technology?

46. What is the Republic of South Sudan higher education enrolment capacity? What is the current enrolment level and gross enrolment rate of the age cohort? Is there a higher education development programme?

47. Does the Republic of South Sudan have in place labour laws and an Employment Policy?

48. Is the Republic of South Sudan a member of the ILO?

49. Has the Republic of South Sudan ratified and domesticated the following 8 ILO core Conventions?

50. Is the Republic of South Sudan ready to implement the

programmes of EAC Institutions?

51. How is the Republic of South Sudan Judicial Institutions prepared to refer cases to EACJ for preliminary rulings?

52. Is the Republic of South Sudan ready to submit to the jurisdiction of the EACJ as stipulated in the Treaty?

53. Is the Republic of South Sudan ready to accept the oversight role of EALA in the Community programmes and projects in her territory?

54. Is the Republic of South Sudan ready to comply with the provisions of Article 50 of the Treaty on the Election of members to EALA and develop rules of procedures to that effect?

The above questions were answered in the negotiations in Arusha, Tanzania by the technical team. The negotiations were held on March, May and August 2015. By 15th April 2016, the Heads of States and Governments admitted the Republic of South Sudan to the East African Community and on 6th October 2016 the country deposited the instruments of accession to EAC Secretariat, African Union and other RECs around the world.

Stay of Application

The Republic of South Sudan immediately applied for a stay of application. In the true sense of word, a stay of application is a suspension of a case or a particular proceeding with in a case by a court or a registered organization. In the case of the Republic of South Sudan, a stay of application was requested by the South Sudanese negotiations for five years in the context of the implementation of the protocols. The Treaty of the EAC Article 7 (h) stipulates the operational principle of the community on variable geometry or asymmetry. This principle indicates that each Partner State can implement the Community protocols, programmes and projects on her own requested time. The

Republic of South Sudan was granted three years stay of application. From 6th October 2016 to 6th October 2019. The main reason for the request of stay of application was to allow the Republic of South Sudan to prepare itself for implementation of the EAC protocols by ensuring that all laws are aligned to the EAC laws. Besides, to ensure that the customs officers and the other officers from other departments of the government were trained and coached on EAC protocols, programmes, projects and activities. However, South Sudan is yet to implement the protocols of EAC in full. The stay of application was granted to the Republic of Burundi and Republic of Rwanda as well from 2007 to 2009 when both countries commenced implementing the EAC protocols.

South Sudanese Technical Negotiators during a
briefing in EAC Secretariat HQs in Arusha, Tanzania.

Republic of Rwanda negotiators during
negotiation in EAC HQ's in Arusha, Tanzania

From right, the author, next to him Dr. James Alic Garang and next Late Hon. Martin Mou Mou Athian Kuol, former Undersecretary of EAC Affairs of the Republic of South Sudan and to the extreme left is a Senior Customs Officer-Republic of South Sudan during negotiations in Arusha-Tanzania.

Republic of South Sudan Technical Negotiation Committee with Technical Negotiators from the five EAC Partner States during the conclusion of negotiations on 30th August 2015 at the EAC HQs in Arusha-Tanzania.

CHAPTER SEVEN

Pre- and Post-South Sudan
Accession Activities

Various activities were carried out before and after the Accession of South Sudan to the East African Community. These activities include sensitization and trainings of the South Sudanese public and those working in the governmental departments.

Pre-South Sudan Accession Activities

Sensitizations and Trainings by EAC Officials

The EAC Secretariat visited Juba in January and February 2015 and commenced sensitizing South Sudanese government officials about the benefits and costs of being in the EAC. The sensitization on the three protocols: Customs Union, Common Market and Monetary Union were discussed. The EAC Secretariat presented the last stage of the EAC integration, Political Federation to the officials from all the departments of the governments..These departments were divided into: security, public administration, economic and social clusters and the trainings covered all those ministries' and institutions.

The Author at the EAC HQ's in Arusha, Tanzania during the second phase of the negotiation of the Republic of South Sudan to the EAC in May 2015

Sensitizations and Trainings by Imani Development Firm

The then Secretary General, Late Martin Mou Mou Athian Kuol with the support from Trademark East Africa (TMEA) contracted Imani Development that carried out a study of pros and cons of South Sudan Accession to the East African Community. Imani Development then organized various workshops for the selected government technical negotiators for South Sudan Accession to the EAC.

Imani Development Impacted the below key ideas on the South Sudanese Focal Persons on EAC Integration

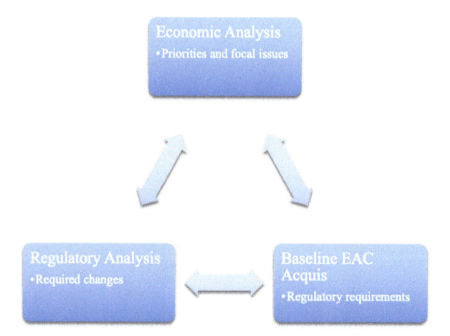

Private Sector Awareness

- Integral part of economic analysis
- But needs to be more explicitly addressed

Negotiating Strategy

- Flexibility (S & DT, Variable Geometry and Speed)
- Experience of Rwanda and Burundi
- Economic arguments

Focus

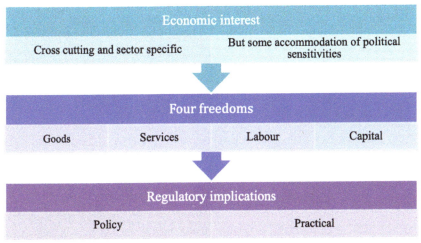

Source: *Imani Development, 2015*

Removal of Non-Trade Barriers (NTBs)

As discussed earlier, NTBs are detrimental to any trade in a country. For the case of EAC, NTBs have been quite hurdles for smooth trade benefits amongst the partner States.

Potential benefit to South Sudan that is only available within EAC framework is as follows:

- Significant potential to improve governance along the corridors
- Already benefiting as it is learning from EAC Partner States politics and business
- If the time-bound programme on NTBs is given legal teeth then within South Sudan, EAC traders could force action to be taken on NTBs within South Sudan

- It is within South Sudan that most of the traders have reported problems but this in part reflects the dominance of imports.

Technical Challenges for Goods

Certification and SPS/ TBT

- South Sudan does not have a system to certify that products originate in South Sudan (compliance rules of origin).
- Until it does then exporters cannot benefit from duty-free preferences
- Except where rules of origin are not needed. This can be referred to Single Custom Territory (SCT).
- A minimum of two years before this can be in place.
- And challenges of SPS and TBT compliance to be met for market access to be effective.

Post-South Sudan Accession Activities

These activities involve trainings on the EAC protocols, programmes and projects on South Sudan and the benefits South Sudanese could acquire from the integration. The Ministry of East African Affairs organized the trainings with funding from Integrate Consulting. The trainings were divided into sessions. The first session was covering the senior civil servants drawn from governance, public administration, economic, infrastructure and social sectors, and different ministries. It was carried out between 4th-11th March 2019 at Palm Africa Hotel. Agenda and topics covered are noted below.

Agenda for the Training of South Sudanese Civil Servants

Drawn from Governance, Public Admiration, Economic and Social Clusters regarding East African Community Issues

Date: 4th-11th March 2019

Venue: Palm Africa Hotel, Juba, South Sudan

TIME	ACTIVITY	FACILITATOR
Day 1		
9:00 – 9:30	Registration	
09.30 – 09.50am	☐ Welcoming by Mou Mou Athian Kuol, Secretary General, South Sudan Secretariat for EAC.	
09.50 – 10.20am	☐ Introduction and plan for the Training ☐ Introducing the Trainers and introduction by the participants. ☐ Overview of EAC Issues	Dr. Tomasz Iwanow
10.20 – 11.00am	☐ Introduction to Regional Integration ☐ Introduction to Regional Integration in Africa ☐ Introduction to East African Integration – the History	Dr. Jacob Dut Chol
11.00 – 11.20am	**Tea Break**	
11.20 – 12.00pm	☐ General overview of the East African Community ☐ Introduction to the Law of the East African Community – the EAC Treaty and other ☐ How the EAC Works: Role, Capacity and Interaction of EAC Organs and Institutions	Mr. Charles Data

12:00-12:30	☐ Questions, answers, discussions on issues mentioned todate.	
12:30-14:00	**Lunch**	
14:00-14:30	☐ East African Court of Justice	Dr. Tomasz Iwanow
14:30-15:00	☐ East African Legislative Assembly	Mr. Ahmed Morgan
15:00 – 15:20	**Coffee/Tea Break**	
15:20 – 15:50	☐ EAC Customs Union Protocol and Implications for South Sudan	Mr. Charles Data
15.50 – until close	Questions, Answers, Discussion	
Day 2		
9:30 – 10:10	☐ EAC Common Market and Implications for South Sudan	Mr. Ahmed Morgan
10:10-10:30	**Tea/Coffee Break**	
10:30-11:00	☐ EAC Monetary Union Market Protocol and implications for East Africa/South Sudan	Mr. Ahmed Morgan
11:00 – 11:30	☐ The Journey Towards the East African Political Federation	Dr. Jacob Dut Chol
11:30 – 12:15	☐ EAC Projects and Programs in the specific area of work of the Ministry being trained	Dr. Tomasz Iwanow
12:15 – 12:30	☐ Questions, Answers, Discussion	
12:30-14:00	Lunch	
14:00-14:30	☐ EAC law and national law: the interactions and co-dependencies	Prof. Tomasz Milej

14:30–15:00	▢ The System of legal protection within the EAC within the context of accession of South Sudan to the Regional Bloc	Prof. Tomasz Milej
15:00–15:20	Tea Break	
15:20–until close	▢ Questions, Answers, Discussion	

The second session for training was rolled out on 22ⁿᵈ–23ʳᵈ July 2019 and was focused on senior civil servants from security sector institutions drawn from Ministries of Defense, Interior, South Sudan People's Defense Forces, National Police Service, National Security Service, National Prison Service, National Wildlife Service and the Civil Defense Service amongst other security organs. The agenda and topics covered are noted in the next page.

Agenda for the Seminar for South Sudan Security Institutions Regarding East African Community Issues

Date: 22nd-23rd July 2019
Venue: Palm Africa Hotel, Juba, South Sudan

TIME	ACTIVITY	FACILITATOR
Day 1		
9:00am – 9:30	Registration	
09.30 - 09.50am	▢ Welcome by Mou Mou Athian Kuol, Secretary General, South Sudan Secretariat for EAC.	
09.50 - 10.20am	▢ Introduction and plan for the Training ▢ Introducing the Trainers and introduction by the participants. ▢ Overview of EAC Issues	Dr. Tomasz Iwanow
10.20 - 11.00am	▢ Introduction to Regional Integration ▢ Introduction to Regional Integration in Africa ▢ Introduction to East African Integration - the History	Dr. Jacob Dut Chol
11.00 – 11.20am	**Tea Break**	
11.20 - 12.00pm	▢ General overview of the East African Community ▢ Introduction to the Law of the East African Community - the EAC Treaty and other ▢ How the EAC Works: Role, Capacity and Interaction of EAC Organs and Institutions	Mr. Charles Data

12:00–12:30	☐ Questions, answers, discussions on issues mentioned to date.	
12:30–14:30	**Lunch**	
14:30–15:00	☐ East African Legislative Assembly	Dr. Ahmed Morgan
15:00 – 15:20	**Coffee/Tea Break**	
15:20 – 15:50	☐ EAC Customs Union Protocol and Implications for South Sudan	Mr. Charles Data
15.50 – until close	Questions, Answers, Discussion	
Day 2		
9:30 – 10:10	☐ EAC Common Market and Implications for South Sudan	Dr. Ahmed Morgan
10:10–10:30	**Tea/Coffee Break**	
10:30–11:00	☐ EAC Monetary Union Market Protocol and implications for East Africa/South Sudan	Dr. Ahmed Morgan
11:00 – 11:30	☐ The Journey Towards the East African Political Federation	Dr. Jacob Dut Chol
11:30 – 12:15	☐ EAC Projects and Programs in the specific area of work of the Ministry being trained.	Dr. Tomasz Iwanow
12:15 – 12:30	☐ Questions, Answers, Discussion	
12:30–14:00	Lunch	
14:00–14:30	☐ EAC law and national law: the interactions and co-dependencies	Prof. Tomasz Milej

14:30–15:00	☐ The System of legal protection within the EAC within the context of accession of South Sudan to the Regional Bloc	Prof. Tomasz Milej
15:00–15:20	Tea Break	
15:20–untill close	☐ Questions, Answers, Discussion	

CHAPTER EIGHT

South Sudan and EAC Private Sector

A dynamic private sector is an integral component of economic growth within any given region. It greatly contributes to employment creation, provision of goods and services, revenue flows and overall poverty reduction. Within Africa, the private sector generates about two thirds of the continent's investment. That is about 75% of its economic output and more than 90% of its formal and informal employment. The EAC recognizes the significance of the private sector and identifies it as the Community's engine towards economic growth. Article 7 (a) of the EAC Treaty articulates that the community should be people-centered and market driven cooperation. This therefore means that private sector is key in driving the integration of the East African region.

Article 127 of the EAC Treaty stipulates that the partner states should agree to provide an enabling environment for the private sector and the civil society to take full advantage of the Community. To this end, the partner states should undertake to formulate a strategy for the development of the private sector and to:

- Promote a continuous dialogue with the private sector and civil society at the national level and at that of the Community to help create an improved business environment for the implementation of agreed decisions in all economic sectors; and

- Provide opportunities for entrepreneurs to participate actively in improving the policies and activities of the institutions of the Community that affect them so as to increase their confidence in policy reforms and raise the productivity and lower the costs of the entrepreneurs.

For purposes of bullet number 1 of this article, the Partner States undertake to:

- Improve the business environment through the promotion of conducive investment codes, the protection of property rights and other rights and the proper regulation of the private sector;
- Stimulate market development through infrastructural linkages and the removal of barriers and constraints to market development and production;
- Regularly provide up-to-date commercial intelligence to speed up market response through co-operation among the chambers of commerce and industry and other similar organizations of the Partner States;
- Facilitate and support the exchange of experience and the pooling of resources through, inter alia, cross-border investments;
- Strengthen the role of their national business organizations or associations in the formulation of their economic policies; and
- Collaborate with their national chambers of commerce and industry to establish lending institutions that shall primarily cater for the private sector especially the small-scale entrepreneurs who find it difficult to obtain credit from commercial banks and financing institutions.

On the other hand, Article 128 of the EAC Treaty further stipulates strengthening the Private Sector as follows:

- The partner states shall endeavor to adopt programmes that would strengthen and promote the role of the private sector as an effective force for the development of their respective economies;
- For purposes of bullet 1 of this Article, the Partner States undertake to: encourage the efficient use of scarce resources and to promote the development of private sector organizations which are engaged in all types of economic activity, such as, the chambers of commerce and industry, confederations and associations of industry, agriculture, manufacturers, farmers, traders, and service providers and professional groups.

East African Business Council (EABC)

The Community has set up mechanisms to include the private sector in its decisions making processes and activities. Such mechanisms include East African Business Council (EABC) that promotes, coordinates and provide platforms for the growth of businesses across the East African region. The EABC does numerous advocacies on behalf of private sector or business associations of East Africa region so that the partner states listen and provide environment for ease doing business in the region. Drawn from business associations or unions of six partner states, EABC has endeavored to sensitize the businessmen and women of East African region to pick opportunities in doing business.

However, EABC has been confronted by some pertinent challenges. These conundrums include, firstly, a lack of constant sources of funding, as many business entities don't remit their annual membership fees. Secondly, the poor formation of business associations or unions at the Partner States levels. This has seriously impacted negatively in the growth and activities of EABC in the partner states. Many business associations, particularly, in Burundi, Uganda, DR Congo and South Sudan faced intermittent infightings that has crippled the proper functioning of these business associations and unions. One of the key issues is the leadership wrangle as most of these business associations and unions are politicized and thus are not operating as private in nature. During elections, the Presidents and Chairpersons are dragged into politics to funds and campaigns for their preferred candidates. This has affected the business objective of these associations and unions or chambers of commerce.

South Sudan Private Sector

The private sector growth and development in South Sudan is still nascent. During the time of the liberation struggle, private sector development was anchored on the Civil Authority of New Sudan (CANS). CANS was able to support many companies that were hailed from the southern part of Sudan. The SPLA commanders and few of civilians owned majority of these companies. After the independence of South Sudan on 9th July 2011, the growth of the private sector was envisaged to take place. However, the 15th December 2013 civil war occurred and this took the young state back to square one. The development of the private sector was then severely affected. With the revitalized of the peace deal known as the Revitalized Agreement on the Resolution of the Conflict in the Republic of South Sudan (R-ARCSS), hopes for the development of the private sector were ignited.

The Role of Women in Business in East African Community

Article 122 of EAC has recognized the importance of women as a vital economic link between agriculture, industry and trade, the Partner States undertake to:

a. Increase the participation of women in business at the policy formulation and implementation levels;

b. Promotes special programmes for women in small, medium and large scale enterprises;

c. Eliminate all laws, regulations and practices that hinder women's access to financial assistance including credit;

d. Initiate changes in educational and training strategies to enable women to improve their technical and industrial employment levels through the acquisition of transferable skills offered by various forms of vocational and on-the-job training schemes; and

e. Recognize and support the national and regional associations of women in business established to promote the effective participation of women in the trade and development activities of the Community.

Representation of Private Sector in South Sudan

Three major institutions in South Sudan represent the private sector. They include: business unions, chambers of commerce, agriculture, trade and industry, and the private sector alliance of South Sudan. While the above three institutions represent businessmen and women in South Sudan, they have never united for the interests of the development of the South Sudanese private sector. The business union believes that it is the right institution to drive the private sector growth and development in the country. On the other hand, the chamber of commerce, agriculture, trade and industry claims that it has the legal mandate to represent the business community in South Sudan. Nonetheless, the private sector alliance of South Sudan positions itself as the proper institution to take charge of the private businesses in the country. Hence, the activities of business community have reached a cul-de-sac in South Sudan.

Lack of East African Business Council (EABC) Representation in South Sudan

Because of the wrangles over power, leadership and recognition, the EABC does not have its presence and footprints in South Sudan. At the 20th July 2022, the High Level Summit on Common Market, and subsequent Summit of Heads of States and Governments on the 21st July 2022, the South Sudanese business community was not represented when hundreds of representatives from other Partner States were. While the author was invited as an expert on regional integration and subsequently attended the dinner of EABC, the author felt that the South Sudan private sector should do more; put aside their differences and unite for the interest of South Sudan as a country as well as for the interests of the citizens and the region.

CHAPTER NINE

"You Don't Dictate The Tune":
The Parasitic Bloc, EAC and EU Relations

Concept of Parasitism

Parasitism biologically refers to an inharmonious inter-specific ecological interaction in which individuals or species (the parasites) use the organs, tissues or cells of individuals of another species (the hosts), causing them harm. Studies of parasite community ecology are often descriptive, focusing on patterns of parasite abundance across host populations rather than on the mechanisms that underlie interactions within a host (Amy and Fenton, 2006). The most common interaction networks in community ecology are consumption webs, which incorporate explicit trophic structure and directionality such that primary producers (basal level) are consumed by species at the intermediate level, which are in turn, consumed by predators higher up the network. I suggest that within–host parasite communities can be represented in a similar fashion, incorporating trophic structure in terms of the resources of the host that the parasites consume and the components of the immune response of the host that attack infecting parasites.

The resource base is the host, a critical variable necessary for understanding parasitic communities. Competition and commensalism are common and mutualists frequently mediate the host-parasitic interaction, as predation is an integral part of transmission in many animal parasitic systems (Price, 1990). In addition to tight linkage in consumption involving parasites, the component communities of one host frequently have cross-linkage into other component communities on other hosts. Therefore, host associations are crucial to understanding parasite communities but also parasite communities profoundly influence host interactions.

One major difficulty with describing within-host parasitic communities is how to estimate interaction longevity strengths. There are several analytical tools in community ecology that enable interaction strengths and network structure to be determined from a range of semi-quantitative and qualitative data (Gotelli and Alison, 2006).

With this parasitic concept, it is appropriate to argue that EAC relations with EU are pivotally built on parasitism. EU funded 15.3% of the EAC budget for 2014/2015 and 14.1% of EAC budget for 2015/2016 and 4.5% for 2016/2017 Fiscal Year. Apart from Budgetary support, the EU has allocated 85 million Euros for a development fund to the EAC. This is 400% to that of EAC members' budgetary contributions. This is quite substantial and can only be done by a true friendly bloc. Moreover, the EU has continued to earmark technical support towards the EAC secretariat and other arms of the Community. Yet, the EAC is stuck in parasitism, not able to reciprocate in kind and action. All EAC-EU supports are path-dependent and tilted to EAC as recipient. Although the EU has benefited from trade of goods from EAC Partner States, the trade relation has been on "whoever pays the piper dictates the tune," making this relations more parasitic. The EAC becomes the parasite, as the EU remains the host.

EU Substantial Budgetary Supports to EAC

As argued earlier, the EAC has continued to depend on financial support from the EU. Substantive budgetary cushions have emanated from the EU and continued to support EAC programmes. The following Table 11 provides insights into the EU contributions.

Table 12: East African Community Secretariat Budget

East African Community Secretariat Budget (USD)	EU Contribution	Actual Partners Contributions	EU Contribution in Percentage
FY'14/15 (1st Jul 2014 to 30 June 2015)	4,329,646	28,115,000	15.3
FY'15/16 (1st Jul 2015 to 30 June 2016)	3,610,260	25,550,220	14.1
FY'16/17 (1st Jul 2016 to 30 June 2017)★	1,018,574	22,500,940	4.5
TOTAL	8,958,480	76,166,160	11.3

Source: EAC Secretariat, Directorate of Finance

Created in 1957 by the Treaty of Rome and launched in 1959, the European Development Fund (EDF) is the EU's main instrument for providing development aid to African, Caribbean and Pacific (ACP) countries and to overseas countries and territories (OCTs).

The EDF funds cooperation activities in the fields of economic development, social and human development as well as regional cooperation and integration. It is financed by direct contributions from EU Member States according to a contribution key and is covered by its own financial rules. Although the 11thEDF remains outside of the EU budget, the negotiations in the Council of Ministers on the different elements of the 11th EDF have taken place in parallel with the negotiations of the external instruments financed under the budget, to ensure consistency. The total financial resources of the 11th EDF amount to 30.5 billion for the period of 2014-2020.

In the field of the external actions of the European Union, the applicable legislation is composed, in particular, by the International Agreement of Cotonou for the aid financed from the European Development Fund, by the basic regulations related to the different cooperation programmes adopted by the Council and the European Parliament, and by the financial regulations.

On the budgetary support, the EU and partners are at the 11th EDF. The 11th EDF was created by an intergovernmental agreement signed in June 2013 – as it is not part of the EU Budget – and entered into force on the 1st March 2015, after ratification by all member states. In order to ensure continuity of funding for cooperation with ACPs and OCTs, a 'Bridging Facility' was set-up to cover the period between the end of the 10th EDF (December 2013) and the start of the 11th EDF (March 2015). This 'Bridging Facility' ceased to exist when the 11th EDF entered into force.

The EU has allocated to the EAC Secretariat 85, 000,000 euros under the European Development Fund (EDF) 11 (EAC Secretariat Report, 2017). This amount is yet to be fully allocated to projects to be implemented at Partner States levels although some amount will be spent at the EAC Secretariat for coordination.

EU Trade with EAC

In the developed world and advanced developing countries, welfare systems are, to a greater or lesser extent, capable of compensating and retooling the slow ones. Welfare systems are absent in Africa, with the possible exception of South Africa. That points to the need for development partners to step in, in this case the EU, with an appropriately designed and sustainable aid-for-trade package. That in turn brings the spotlight back to the aid for trade agenda. A far-sighted view on the EU's part would recognize that this might be a small price to pay for politically stable, reforming, and ultimately expanding economies that will become larger markets for European exports and investment. The value of total trade flows between the EAC and the twenty seven EU members states is about 0.12% of EU imports; exports to the EU being dominated by a few products such as plants, flowers, coffee, vegetables, fish and tobacco. The EU mainly exports machinery, chemicals and vehicles to the EAC.

Implications of EPAs to the EAC

EPAs are Economic Partnerships Agreements that have been negotiated and signed by EU with Africa and Caribbean countries. Since 2002, the East African Community (EAC) Partner States of Burundi, Kenya, Rwanda, Tanzania and Uganda have been negotiating an Economic Partnership Agreement (EPA) with the European Union (EU). The EPAs negotiations were finalized on 16th October 2014. It was then signed by Kenya and Rwanda in September 2016 and Kenya went ahead and ratified it. Uganda and Tanzania have reservations on the document. However, Burundi was sanctioned by the EU and thus could not trade directly or through the EAC with the EU. Hence, Burundi has not inked the EPA. However, while the new President is now normalizing Burundi relations with European Union. his efforts are yet to reap some fruits. Other Partner States of EAC are members of World Trade Organization (WTO) except South Sudan. Being a member of the WTO is quite critical for the enhancement of borderless trade and moreover helps a country to derive benefits from trade.

Although the EAC-EU EPAs covers several cooperation areas of interest to the EAC and EU economies such as development matters, the main objective of cooperation in goods trade is the liberalization of trade between the two regions. For a long time trade between EAC Partner States and EU member countries was governed by the African Caribbean Pacific (ACP) group of countries. The EU Agreement trading regime, the ACP-EU trading regime provided un-reciprocal market access to EU products exported from the ACP countries, with exports from the former (including EAC partner states) entering the EU market on duty-free basis, while exports from the EU to EAC countries were subjected to import duty. Once negotiations are completed and once the agreement comes into force, the EAC-EU EPA will provide a reciprocal preferential trading arrangement between EAC Partner States and the EU member countries (Mbithi, 2015). EAC's liberalization of EU imports is progressive; starting two years after the EAC-EU EPA comes into effect with import duty being targeted for elimination within a period of 17 years after the EAC- EU EPA comes into effect (EAC, 2008).

The EPAs on EU and EAC are argued on potential positive and negative implications; Monica Hangi (2009) argues that the EPA will lead to a closer economic integration between East African countries and the EU; thereby enlarging the market for these countries (Hangi, 2009). This enlarged market, governed by a stable, transparent and predictable framework for trade, will allow for economies of scale, improve the level of specialization, reduce production and transaction costs and altogether help to increase competitiveness. This will lead to an increase in trade flows, technology and investment in the country and hence promote sustainable development and contribute to poverty reduction. The EAC Customs Union will also get a positive boost from EPA negotiations and regarding the Common External Tariff, final solutions will be easily obtained once member countries sign EPA with the EU.

The EPA will contribute to trade policy reforms within the member countries, introducing increased openness as well as transparency. The EPA will consolidate and lock in these reforms, thereby making these policies more predictable and less reversible. This will help to mobilize economic operators and to attract foreign investment.

EPAs negatively impacts on the EU-EAC trade of goods and services, and particularly on EU-EAC members States. The loss of government revenue is taken, as a short term and static consequence of EPA since long term, more dynamic consequences, are more important. These long-term dynamic effects such as economies of scale, increased efficiency, and productivity changes are a result of greater competition, as mentioned above. An increased unemployment rate is as well anticipated which will at the end provoke economic insecurity and political instability within the region.

Due to the EPAs, the provision of health, education and other basic social services will only be available to those who can pay for them. Low-income groups, the peasants and the unemployed will have less access to fewer basic social services; and the dumping of cheap EU agricultural surpluses (dairy products, cereals, beef, etc.) is seen as a threat to the viability of agriculture and agri-processing industries, particularly for the small scale farming sectors, which does not receive state support. Rural economies will collapse hence increasing insufficiency and food insecurity.

Changing Global Order and Effects on EAC-EU Relations

The changes in European integration with Brexit, coupled with global pressures such as migration, climate change and terrorism, are likely to change the relationship between the EAC-EU, particularly, the EAC's financial dependency. This should be born in mind insofar as how much the funding the EAC has been receiving from the EU could be scaled down. The UK has averaged around 12 billion in the

EU funding each year between 2011-2015 but over that same period made an average net contribution of 15 billion. It is Germany that takes the lead in funding the EU budget with an annual average of around 15 billion (Dieter and Higgott, 2003). Since Britain pulled out of the EU single market, it funding to the EU has ceased and thus the overall funding of the EU has dropped and consequently this has affected the EAC budgetary and development support.

Migration has been a seriously debated issue amongst the European Union members' states. While some members feel that free flows and movement of people should be restricted due to the immigrants' constraint of resources to the migrating countries together with security threats, other members believe that migration is part and parcel of the human integration. This debate has arisen often, fuelled by terrorists attack in France, Brussels and United Kingdom. A key finding and policy implication of the research is that restrictive immigration policies are not effective in deterring or containing migration (EC Report, 2016). Instead, they simply increase the costs and risks of movement, including through exposing people to exploitation by smugglers and traffickers, as well as employers in places of destination. Moreover, research has suggested that restrictive policies also reduce return migration, as immigrants feel 'trapped' in their country of immigration and are reluctant to risk leaving in case they are unable to re-enter (UNCTAD Report, 2009). Thus policies aimed at promoting return should regularize the situation of migrants, enabling them to move freely and safely between countries of destination and origin.

However, apart from restrictive migration policy to Europe, the migration policy to the U.S. during President Trump time was more restrictive. President, Donald J. Trump was anti-immigration and anti-globalization and fighting for free immigration was a daunting task during his time. Yet, the current President, Joe Biden is a liberal leader. Several European countries such as Belgium, Italy, Hungary, Spain and Greece have been supporting anti-immigration policies and if not reversed, the entire EU could be infected with these policies. This could affect the EAC-EU relations immensely since migration of EAC citizens to EU member States is very high and frequent. The same applies to the EU citizens travelling to the EAC Partner States for commerce and tourism. It is upon Germany and France to continue their of the European Union.

CHAPTER TEN

Re-Engineering the EAC Protocols
for Timely Implementation

The Concept of Re-engineering

The concept of re-engineering traces its origins back to management theories developed as early as the nineteenth century. The purpose of reengineering is to make all your processes the 'best in class.' Frederick Taylor suggested in the 1880s that managers could discover the best processes for performing work and reengineer them to optimize productivity. It echoes the classical belief that there is one best way to conduct tasks in a society. In Taylor's time, technology did not allow large companies to design processes in a cross-functional or cross-departmental manner (Taylor, 1886). Specialization was the state-of-the-art method to improve efficiency given the technology of the time.

In the early 1900s, Henry Fayol applied this concept of re-engineering. He argues that this re-engineering helped to conduct the undertaking toward its objectives by seeking to derive optimum advantage from all available resources and options (Fayol, 1908). Although the technological resources of our era have changed, the concept still holds. About the same time, another business engineer, Lyndall Urwick, (1942) stated that it is not enough to hold people accountable for certain activities, it is also essential to delegate to them the necessary authority to discharge that responsibility as you the leader socially engineer a society (Urwick, 1942). This description showcases the idea of worker empowerment, which is central to reengineering.

Although William Hammer and Andrea Champy (1980) declare that classical organization theory is obsolete, classical ideas such as division of labor have had an enduring power and applicability that re-engineering has so far failed to demonstrate as 'the best in class' (Hammer and Champy, 1980). Re-engineering in management does not appear to qualify as a scientific theory, because, among other things, it is not duplicable and it has limited scope in coverage and in time. The applicability of classical management theories, such as division of labor, lands as a means of production etc., were widely duplicable and portable. These ideas stimulated increases in productivity, output, and income that led to the creation of the middle class.

According to Thomas Davenport (1960) classical reengineering repeats the same mistakes as the classical approach to management by separating the design of work from its execution (Davenport, 1960). Typically, a small re-engineering team, often from outside the company, designs work for the many. The team is fueled by assumptions such as there is one best way to organize work. "I can easily understand how you do your work today; I can design your work better than you can; there is little about your work now that is worth saving; you will do your work the way I specify" (Davenport, 1960). Davenport further suggests that the engineering model/analogy that the theory is based upon is flawed, both in terms of process design and information technology (Ibid). He proposes an "ethnographic" approach to process design and an "ecological" approach to information systems. However, re-engineering has remained a popular concept and theory for the best design in industrial and social engineering.

From the understanding of the concept of re-engineering as explained above and which basically refers to the best way of doing things, it is imperative that a re-engineering of the protocols is urgently needed to achieve deeper integration and wider cooperation.

Sequencing of Re-engineering of EAC Protocols

Today if the re-engineering of the EAC protocols was to begin the adoption and implementation of the protocols from Political Federation, followed by Common Market, Monetary Union and finally Customs Union, then deeper integration would be experienced in the East African region. Why should the protocols begin with Political Federation? This is because politics is the ultimate driver of other sectors. If it is politics stupid now! Then it can consequently be economic and social stupid! That means if politics is run badly in the region, then economic will turn bad too as political decisions affect economic policies. This also applies to social policies, which are equally affected by political decisions. Hence, politics include influencing of decisions and actions and thus activities can take place in that particular polity base on certain political decisions. If the EAC Partner States would have adopted the Political Federation Protocol, then the region could have been under one political system by now, for instance, political confederation that means policies; programmes and projects could have been easily and keenly supervised and implemented by one central authority. The central authority in this case is the President of the Confederation of East African Community.

European Union (EU) Experience

The European Union (EU) is much younger than the East African Community (EAC) due to its upgrade through the Maastricht Treaty of 1992. Then being conclusively founded via the Lisbon Treaty of 2007 that was entered into in 2009. Because EU member states began their integration with political confederation, their economic and social integration followed. That is why today we have a very influential EU High Representative for Politics, Security and Foreign Affairs that have continued to champion EU politics, security and foreign policy. While the EU has a lot to solidify its political confederation, it has already deepened its integration in economics through Common Market and Customs Unions. Due to its common political system, policies and programmes, the EU is enjoying its substantial integration. The movement of people and labour due to the Schengen visa is effective and the movements of capital and rights of establishment have already been achieved. Common customs duties and common infrastructure have been attained. This EU integration has demonstrated that engineering the integration with political federation/confederation is a path towards achieving genuine regional integration.

Possible Benefits of South Sudan in the Re-engineered EAC Protocols

South Sudan can benefit a lot if the protocols of the EAC are re-engineered and begin with Political Confederation. The conundrum of South Sudan is one of 'dirty politics.' The political environment in South Sudan is so confused in that the idea 'hygiene' in politics is history. The political and military elites who are the liberators of the nascent state have forgotten the ideals of the taxing liberation wars between Khartoum and themselves. The NCP turncoats and the wartime by-standing Sudanese warlords who were paid peanuts to fight their own brothers and sisters in the South have lost the basic of politics 101 in running the young state. Thus, if protocols of integration are sequenced today to begin with political confederation, South Sudan will be forced to change from 'dirty' politics to transformative politics and visionary democracy as it is being practiced in the region by other countries.

One of the key successes of South Sudan accession to the EAC is the use of the East African Court of Justice (EACJ), both First Instance and Appellate Divisions. Although South Sudan has sent one Judge to the EACJ instead of two, the South Sudanese civil society members have mostly used the court. One of the case and first case after South Sudan's admission to the Community was the un-procedural selection of the nine members of the EALA representing South Sudan. The President of the Republic, Salva Kiir Mayardit decided to hand pick these members contrary to the EAC Treaty Article 50 that stipulates that the nine members shall be elected by the National Assembly. Wani Michael, a member of civil society sued against the un-procedural nomination of the nine members to the EACJ First Instance Division and the ruling was immediately made cancelling all the nominations of President Salva Kiir and making them null and void. President Salva Kiir had no any other option but to abide by the EACJ ruling. Thus, the National Assembly representing different parties elected nine members with the quotas of minorities, youth and women representations.

Another case in point was the un-procedural dismissal of judges in South Sudan, which the EACJ nullified when a case was filed there. Another recent case is the resolution of South Sudan Council of Ministers, No. 39/2021 that authorized dredging of White Nile tributaries by the Republic of Egypt without credibility studies on the environment and ecology. That resolution was challenged and the EACJ nullified the resolution forcing President Salva Kiir to cancel the dredging activities until the Ministry of Environment carries out scientific and credible studies on environment. So far, the services of EACJ have been widely used by South Sudanese and this is a great transformative journey South Sudanese citizens have been dreaming of having a country, which is ruled by the rule of law and a country where the Head of State and Government doesn't easily abrogates the laws that he has overseen being enacted by the national legislatures.

Possible Conundrums of South Sudan in the Re-engineered EAC Protocols

The same problems South Sudan have experienced in deepening its integration will continue in the re-engineered EAC protocols for fast-track integration. These problems include delays in harmonization and aligning of South Sudanese laws, regulations and policies into the EAC regional laws, regulations and policies. Besides, challenges such as delay in payment of annual subscription fees to the EAC Secretariat will continue. Currently, South Sudan has up to 39 USD as the outstanding fees that it should pay in 2022. This is an accumulated arrears of four and half years the nascent Republic has not paid to the EAC. If the Government of the Republic of South Sudan doesn't pay its 8 million USD subscription fee in 2022, then South Sudan shall have accumulated arrears totaling to 47 million (USD) by 2023. This is a dangerous trend for the Republic of South Sudan, which will prevent the young state to participate in the EAC programmes and projects. So far there have been a lot of lamenting and insults by the members of the East African Legislative Assembly (EALA) from Partner States who view South Sudanese leaders as not ready to integrate the country to into the Community. The members of EALA from Partner States went as far as insulting South Sudanese as people who don't understand anything in their lives except violence and wars. These insults were filmed and can be found on the Internet for any one to watch and digest. While the South Sudanese government feels that it doesn't warrant such insults, the nascent state should play its key roles in the integration. Otherwise, it risks forfeiting it membership through expulsion from the EAC as stipulated in the EAC Treaty Article 147.

REFERENCES

Adams, C. (1993). *Black Slavery and Its Impacts in USA.* University of Washington Press.

Arad and Arye L. (1979). "Embargo Threat, Learning and Departure from Comparative Advantage," *Journal of International Economics* 9 (May): 265-75.

Asante-Poku, A and Angelucci, F. (2013). "Analysis of Incentives and Disincentives for Cocoa in Ghana." *Technical Notes Series,* Monitoring African Food and Agricultural Policies (MAFAP) Project. Rome: MAFAP-Food and Agriculture Organization.

Balistei, A. (2014). *Trade Costs in Sub-Saharan Africa.* Princeton Press.

Bernal, L. (1998). The Integration of Small Economies in the Free Trade Area of the Americas. *Policy Papers* on the Americas, Volume IX, Study 1, CSIS Americas Program.

Bhalla, A. and Bhalla P. (1997). *Regional Blocs.* Macmillan Press Ltd., London. Blanchard, Olivier Jean and Katz, Lawrence F. "Regional Evolutions." Brookings Papers

Buyonge, A and Kireeva, B. (2008). *Challenges of Trade Policies Implementation in Africa.* City Printers

Byron, J. (1994) "CARICOM in the Post-Cold War Era: Regional Solutions or Continued Regional Contradictions ?" *Working Paper Series* No. 178, Institute of Social Studies, The Hague, The Netherlands.

Capoccia, G. and Ziblatt, D. (2010). "The Historical Turn in Democratization Studies: A New Research Agenda for Europe and Beyond." *Comparative Political Studies* 43: 931-968.

Chan, D. (1984). "Mirror, Mirror on the Wall ... Are the Freer Countries More Pacific?" *Journal of Conflict Resolution* 28: 617-48.

Collier, P. et al. (1997) "The Future of Lomé: Europe's Role", *The World Economy, Vol. 20* (3): 285-306.

Council of the European Union (1998) "Negotiating Directives for the Negotiation of a Development Partnership Aagreement with the ACP Countries". *Information Note.* 10017/98, European Union, Brussels.

Davenport, T. (1960). *The Mistakes of Classical Re-engineering Theory.* Wilmer Publishing House.

Dewi F. 1994. *Indonesia in ASEAN. Foreign Policy and Regionalism.* St. Martin's Press. New York.

Dieter, H. and Higgott, R. (2003). "Exploring Alternative Theories of Economic Regionalism: From Trade to Finance in Asian Co-operation?" *Review of International Political Economy* 10: 430-454

Drysdale, P. and Gamaut, R. (1992). *The Pacific: An Application of a General Theory of Economic Integration.* Presented at the Twentieth Pacific Trade and Development

Duchene, F. (1994). *The First Statesman of Interdependence.* Norton: New York.

Conference, Washington, DC.

EAC Secretariat *Report,* 2017

European Commission (2016). "Understanding and Tackling the Migration Challenge: The Role of Research," *International Conference Report,* Brussels.

Factsheet on the *Interim of EPA,* 2009.

Fawcett, L. (2004). "Exploring Regional Domains: A Comparative History of Regionalism." *International Affairs,* 80: 429-446.

Fayol, H. (1908). *The Application of Re-engineering Theory in Organizations.* Legend Publishers.

Fishlow, A. and Haggard, S. (1992). "The United States and the Regionalization of the World Economy", *OECD Development Centre Research Project on Globalization and Regionalization,* Paris: OECD Publishing

Giordano, B. (2000). Italian Regionalism or 'Padanian' Nationalism-the Political Project of the Lega Nord in Italian Politics. *Political Geography* 19: 445–47

Gotelli, N. and Allison A. (2006). Food Web Models Predicts Species Abundances in Response to Habitat Changes. <u>*Plos Biol,*</u> 4 (2006): 1869-1873

Hammer, W and Champy, A. (1980). *The Obsolete of the Organizational Theory.* Macmillan Publishers.

Hangi, M. (2009). "EU-EAC Economic Partnership Agreements Negotiations: Current Status," *The Economic and Social Research Foundation (ESRF).*

Hanson G. and Harrison A. (1999). "Trade Liberalisation and Wage Inequality in Mexico," *Industrial and Labor Relations Review,* vol. 52, pp. 271–88

Haas, B. (1958). *The Uniting of Europe.* Stanford University Press

Hartzenberg, T. (2011). Regional Integration in Africa, *Staff Working Paper ERSD-2011-14,* World Trade Organization, Economic Research and Statistics Division.

Hillman, L. and Long. V. (1983). "Pricing and Depletion of an Exhaustible Resource when there is Anticipation of Trade Disruption," *Quarterly Journal of Economics* 98 (May): 215-33.

Hull, C. (1948). *The Memoirs of Cordell Hull.* MacMillan, New York.

Hurrell, A. (1995). *Regionalism in Theoretical Perspective.* In Regionalism in World Politics: Regional Organization and International Order, in L. Fawcett and A. Hurrell (eds). Oxford: Oxford University Press.

IADB. (1995). Economic Integration in the Americas: Periodic Note on Integration. *Online version.*

Inotai, A. (1991). Regional Integration Among Developing Countries, Revisited. *Pre-Working Paper,* WPS 643.

Irwin, D. (1992). Multilateral and Bilateral Trade Policies in the World Trading System: A Historical Perspective," in J. de Melo and A. Panagariya (eds.). *New Dimensions in Regional Integration,* Cambridge University Press.

Jones, M. (1983). *The Limits of Liberty.* Thomson Litho Ltd, East Kilbride, Scotland.

Jordan, R. (1969). *The Civil War.* National Geographic Special Publications Division. Third printing 1975.

Julian, K. (2012). African Integration and Inter-Regionalism: The Regional Economic Communities and their Relationship with the European Union." *Review for Southern Africa* 34, no. 1: 328-351

Kafeero, A. (2008). *ICT Systems and Clearance at Border Posts.* East African Publishers.

Kant, I. (1992). *Perpetual Peace. A Philosophical Essay.* Thoemmes Press, Bristol.

Khaguli, W. (2013). *Impact of Trade Facilitation on Eight Border Posts of Eastern Africa Region.* Red Sea Publishers.

Lee, M. (2002). "Regionalism in Africa: A Part of Problem or a Part of Solution." *Polis/R.C.S.P./ C.P.S.R.* Vol. 9, Numéro Spécial.

Lopez, R and Schiff, M. (1998). Migration and the Skill-Composition of the Labor Force: The Impact of Trade Liberalization in LDCs," *Canadian Journal of Economics, Vol 31* (2), pp. 318-36.

Machlup, F. (1977). *A History of Thought on Economic Integration.* New York: Columbia University Press.

Mansfield, D. (1993). "Effects of International Politics on Regionalism in International Trade", Chapter 9 in K. Anderson and R. Blackhurst, eds. *Regional Integration and the Global Trading System.* New York: St. Martin's Press.

Mbithi M, et al. (2015). "Impact of Economic Partnership Agreements: The Case of EAC's Manufactured Imports from EU", *International Journal of Business and Economic Development._Vol 3*: (2): 67-90

McQueen, M. (1998) "Lomé Versus Free Trade Agreements: The Dilemma Facing the ACP Countries," *The World Economy*, vol.21, no.4, pp. 421-44.

Milward, S. (1992). *The European Rescue of the Nation-State*. Univ. of Cal. Press: Berkeley.

Morrison A. and Zabin, R. (1994). *Two-Step Mexican Migration to the United States: The Role of Mexican Export Agriculture*. Mimeo, Dept. of Economics, Tulane University.

Mugisa, D et al. (2009). Foreign Direct Investment in EAC Markets. East Africa Business Council *Report*.

Mulaudzi, C. (2006) "The Politics of Regionalism in Southern Africa." Institute for Global Dialogue (IGD) *Occasional Paper No 51*. Pretoria, South Africa: IGD.

OECD. (1995). *Regional Integration and Multilateral Trading System: Synergy and Divergence,* OECD, Paris.

Page, S. (1996). Intensity Measures for Regional Groups. *Paper prepared for EADI 9th General Conference*, 11-14 September, Vienna.

Polachek, W. (1992). Conflict and Trade: An Economics Approach to Political Interactions," in W. Isard and C.H. Anderton (eds.) *Economics of Arms Reduction and the Peace Process.* Amsterdam: North Holland, 89-120.

Polachek, W. (1996). "Why Democracies Cooperate More and Fight Less: The Relationship Between International Trade and Cooperation," *Review of International Economics, Vol 5* (3): 295-309.

Price, P. (1990). *Hot Population As Resources Defining Parasite Community Organization*. Chapman and Hall

Rajkanikar, R. (2007). *Implementation of WTO Customs in Nepal*. Universal Press.

Ricupero, R. (1998). What Policy Makers Should Know about Regionalism," *Keynote Address* presented at the World Bank Conference on What Policy Makers Should Know about Regionalism, Geneva.

Sakyi, D & Eric E. (2014). Regionalism and Economic Integration in Africa: A conceptual and Theoretical Perspective. *Occasional Paper No. 22*

Soamiely, A. and Schiff, M. (2000). "Regional Groupings Among Microstates," *Review of International Economics, Vol 2 (3): 151-182*

Salvatore, D. (2010). *International Economics.* Hoboken, New Jersey: John Wiley & Sons, Inc.

Schiff, M. (1998). Ethnic Diversity and Economic Reform in Sub-Sahara Africa," *J. Afr. Econ.* 7 (3): 348-62.

Schiff, M. and Winters, A. (1998). Regional Integration as Diplomacy. *World Bank Economic Review, Vol. 2* (12): 271-296.

Senarclens, P. and A. Kazancigil. (2007). *Regulating Globalization: Critical Approaches to Global Governance.* Tokyo: United Nations University Press.

Sewastynowicz, J. (1986). Two-step Migration and Upward Mobility on the Frontier: the Safety Valve Effect in Pejibaye, Costa Rica," *Ec. Dev. Cul. Change* 34: 731-53

Söderbaum, F. (2004). Modes of Regional Governance in Africa: Neoliberalism, Sovereignty- boosting and Shadow Networks, Global Governance. *Review of Multilateralism and International Organizations* 10: 419-436.

Srinivasan, T.N. 1994. "Regional Trading Arrangements and Beyond. Exploring Some Options for South Asia: Theory, Empirics and Policy," *Report no. IDP-142.* South Asia Region, The World Bank.

Swann, Dennis. 1992. *The Economics of the Common Market.* Harmondsworth, Middlesex, England: Penguin Books

Talbott, S. (1996). Democracy and the national interest." *Foreign Affairs. Vol. 75* (2): 47-63.

Taylor, F. (1886). *Re-engineering Theory for Effective Performance in an Organization.* Palgrave.

Taylor, T. (1979). *Munich: the Price of Peace,* Vintage, New York. Viner, J. 1950. *The Customs Union Issue,* New York: Carnegie Endowment for International Peace.

Trpcevska, P. (2014). Effects on the Implementation of Single Window of Simplified Customs Procedures in Macedonia. Haack Publishers.

United Nations Conference for Trade and Development (UNCTAD) (2009). *Economic Development in Africa Report: Strengthening Regional Economic Integration for Africa's Development.*

Urwick, L. (1942). *Social Engineering of the Society.* Princeton University Press.

Wallace W. (1994) *Regional Integration: The West European Experience,* Brookings, Washington, D.C.

Whalley, J. (1998). "Why Do Countries Seek Regional Trade Agreements?" Chapter 3 in Frankel, J. (ed.) *The Regionalization of the World Economy,* Chicago, Chicago University Press.

Winters L. (1997). What Can European Experience Teach Developing Countries about Integration?" *The World Economy, Vol 20* (14): 889-912.

Winters L. (2001). Post-Lomé Trading Arrangements: the Multilateral Alternative," in von Hagen J and Widgren M (ed.s), *Regionalism in Europe,* Kluwer.

WTO (2005). *Special Report on Global Trading Activities.* WTO Press Unit.

WTO (2021). *Report on Trade and Changing Environment.* WTO Press Unit.

INDEX